DR. HANK SEITZ

THE HAPPIEST MAN
IN THE WORLD

Manifest  Publishing

Copyright © 2016 by Dr. Hank Seitz

All rights reserved worldwide.

No part of this book may be reproduced, redistributed, transmitted, re-transmitted, translated, sold, given away, decompiled or otherwise circumvented by any means, electronic or mechanical, including photocopying, recording, or by any information storage or retrieval system, without written permission from the publisher, Manifest Publishing.

This book is designed to provide information and processes used by Dr. Hank Seitz. Every effort has been made to make it as complete and accurate as possible, but no warranty is implied.

The information in this book is provided on an "as is" basis. Manifest Publishing and the author make no guarantees that you will experience the same results as the author. The author has no responsibility to any person or entity with respect to loss or damage arising from information contained in this book or from any programs or document that may accompany it.

Manifest Publishing
Dallas, Texas
www.manifestpublishing.com

The Happiest Man in the World / Dr. Hank Seitz
ISBN-10: 1-944913-05-X
ISBN-13: 978-1-944913-05-2

"Dr. Hank shares the most fascinating stories of his Life from catching the Korean mafia, working for the CIA and building a million-dollar consulting company."

"*The Happiest Man in the World* showed me how to keep the faith and know that no matter how bad it gets, there is always a way out with God! Dr. Hank even broke his neck and he was able to use this to make himself stronger and healthier!"

"His story is really all of our stories with the trials and tribulations that will turn out for the best when we look for the best. Even in the most difficult of times, God is there to rescue us and take us to an even better place."

"This is the most inspiring book I have ever read and shows the power that lies within each one of us!"

—Paul Bermudez, Top 300 U.S. Real Estate Broker

Contents

Trapped on the Mountaintop of Hell 1

Viva Las Vegas 11

The Power to Create Reality 19

Prepare for Anything 27

If It Moves, Kill It 35

German Bayonet Knife 41

Oh to Be Thirteen 47

The UniBoys 53

Communicating with Source 63

Seeing and Feeling the Love All Around Me 77

My Mother 81

Shifting Momentum to Change Your Life 89

Healing Myself from a Broken Neck 93

You Can Create a New Story 101

    Age Birth to Five 103

    Age Five to 10 103

    Age 10 to 15 104

    Age 15 to 20 104

    Age 20 to 25 105

    Age 25 to 30 105

- Age 30 to 35 106
- Age 35 to 40 107
- Age 40 to 45 108
- Age 45 to 50 108
- Age 50 to 55 109
- Age 55 to 60 110

The Power of Thought and Mindfulness 111

The Joy Shop 119

Top Performers 127

- Thought Success Unit 134
- The Zones Success Unit 136
- Beliefs Success Unit 149
- Prioritize Life Success Unit 151
- Emotional Intelligence Success Unit 151

Becoming the Happiest Person in the World 153

Health and Youthfulness 177

World of Plenty 181

Divine Relationships 199

Healthfulness and Youthfulness 205

Epilogue 225

This book is dedicated to that which is unseen but always felt, who is always here loving us and guiding us on our Lighted path

CHAPTER 1

Trapped on the Mountaintop of Hell

I thought to myself, "What the hell am I doing here? Sitting alone on a mountaintop in South Korea?"

Damn North Koreans.

It was Christmas, and I could hear dozens of enemy MiGs flying overhead. They were messing with us. Messing with me. Messing with us for the sake of messing with us. Why? Because they could. That's why.

Of course, we had our missiles on them, but we couldn't fire at them because that would be an "international scene." We needed permission from the President of the United States before we could do anything like that. That wasn't going to happen.

We were all stuck there like sitting ducks, waiting. Just waiting. However, unlike sitting ducks, we were, each of us, aware of our predators.

Me? I wanted out of there.

Their plan was working. They were driving me crazy. It was enough to drive anyone crazy, really. I knew I was losing my mind. I started to think about all the many things I had done so wrong, and what a mess I had made of my life. I was there alone with all of my guilt, shame, and worthlessness.

Jennifer.

My father.

My brothers.

I knew I deserved this. I believed that I was never going to amount to anything. Never be anything good. Tonight, like every other night since I'd been there, I would cry myself to sleep. Me, a big hairy guy and a Sergeant in the U.S. Army with lots of responsibilities, crying myself to sleep. How pathetic.

I wasn't just afraid of enemy jets flying overhead, I was as much afraid of the day when I would have to go home. So what if the bastards did bomb us? If I did survive this hell hole of a mess, I would have to go home to the humiliation waiting for me there.

Maybe my dad was right.

Maybe James was right.

James, another soldier in my supply office, had his executive father run an extensive detailed background check on me. James told me that it showed I would not amount to anything. Ever. Could this really be true?

It was getting dark. As I listened to the enemy jets fly over, what I heard were the words of so many people I had let down in the last year. I felt helpless and hopeless. I sank into the feeling that I'd never go to college; that I would never get a decent job with any corporation in America. I had screwed up so many things. So many things were wrong. I had made huge mistakes that would never be forgiven.

Crystal Clarity

I returned to my room. I felt desperate, like I was in the Valley of Death. I felt alone, filled with an insane amount of guilt and worthlessness. This was the lowest point I had ever been in my life. I was so down, so sad, so alone, so desperate, and so disempowered—to the point of lifelessness.

I reached under my bed and grabbed my Army-issued .22 caliber pistol. I wasn't willing to live like this anymore. I placed the muzzle to my right temple; I slowly cocked the hammer. The click of the hammer penetrated the darkness. I could hear my own breathing like a freight train. I knew one pull of the trigger and the bullet would shatter my temple, ending the pain and heartache that I no longer wanted to live with. It would be better.

I couldn't do it. I couldn't pull the trigger. Even with a gun to my head, there was still something that was calling me forward into life. I had all of this negativity and guilt, yet there it was, something calling me to live.

I tried to focus again on the gun, on the trigger.

Again, I couldn't do it.

There was something inside of me telling me that this was not right. This was not the answer. I knew that I wanted to live.

Then I had a moment of crystal clarity.

There was no reason to die. It was like they say—in a moment my lifetime flashed by. I saw that none of what I had done—or not done—mattered. I knew that there was more waiting for me in my life ahead. I cautiously cocked the hammer back until it released to safety and put the gun down.

The feeling of pure freedom and joy overtook me. It was as if a thousand pounds melted from my shoulders. I decided that I would stay in this beautiful world.

I was inspired not only to live, but to make the most of every day that I am here.

I discovered faith.

I discovered joy.

I discovered that life is good.

And, I realized that it was only going to get better. I knew that I was destined for more and that life was going to unfold the way I expected.

I decided to enjoy the present moment more. I started looking at the things that were playing out for me. With faith, in knowing that good things would come to me, in moment of clarity, I began a new life.

Getting in Bed with the Korean Mafia

It was a couple of days later when I was approached by Kim, a North Korean in my supply chain, who asked me if I would like to make a bunch of extra money.

I said, "Sure. How?" I had lots of debts to pay back home, and the extra money would help.

He said, "Well, I am connected to the Korean Mafia."

My heart skipped a beat, but I was all ears.

In my job, I was in charge of five supply points including Seoul, Korea. Kim wanted me to run U.S. Army supplies to the Mafia. He told me they would handle all the orders. I would have the Korean-born people working my supply points at all the military sites. He told me their background checks would check out, but they really were more loyal to Korea than to the United States Army.

I said to him, "I would love to make more money and get involved with the Korean Mafia, but I want to see and meet the head of the Mafia first."

He said, "Okay, I'll let you know and get back to you."

It took a couple of weeks, but they finally got everything set up for our meeting. I was picked up in a car with two armed men who acted like bodyguards. We drove the three or four hours down the mountain through the rice paddies and military zones and into Seoul, Korea. It wasn't an easy ride.

We pulled up to the Mafia King's home. Most Koreans were fortunate to live in thatched huts. His home was a small palace compared to how others in South Korea lived. It was loaded with TVs everywhere and other modern appliances. Yet, even though it was filled with luxury, at over six feet tall, I had to duck to go from room to room.

The Mafia King only spoke Korean, and I only spoke English, so we needed an interpreter. Kim, who had originally approached me, was there for that purpose. I was going along with everything the head of the Mafia was asking me to do. I instantly liked him and felt safe. He was a kind and gracious man who made me feel good and relaxed. I was even introduced to his wife and a few children.

He wore a modest suit that fit snugly around his short, portly frame. He reminded me of a jolly kind of guy. Although he was generous and fun with me, I sensed he could be dangerous and was not someone to mess with.

We agreed to take our talks further at a nearby restaurant.

There was one armed car in front of us and one behind us. Our car had two armed guards in the front seat. Kim, the Mafia King, and myself were in the backseat. When we pulled up to the restaurant, the front car of armed men got out, went into the restaurant, and cleared the entire restaurant of people. People were scurrying like little mice out of the restaurant. This was a big deal as it was the head of the Mafia and a United States Soldier doing business together.

When all was clear, the armed guards came and opened the car door for us.

Everyone bowed as we entered. God it was an exciting time! The air was filled with electricity and we laughed, ate, drank, and through the interpreter, had upbeat conversations.

We sat in the middle of the restaurant completely alone. The only ones there were Kim, the interpreter, the Mafia King, myself, the armed guards, the cooks and waiters. I was having a grand time. The dinner was delightful and fun. I ate and drank lots, was laughing, and had a really great time.

After dinner, the Mafia King turned to my interpreter and whispered something. Kim turned to me and said, "He likes you and wants to do business with you."

I was then told how this would roll out. They would handle all the paperwork. I needed only to direct my supply trucks to pick up goods at various U.S. supply points; they would then be directed where to drop off the goods. It was simple. We shook hands and left the restaurant. I was 100% on board all the way.

After dinner on our way back, we drove up a side road and parked next to a building. I could feel a slight twinge of fear creeping up the back of my neck and flushing my face. I had no idea what was about to happen. Much to my relief and surprise, out came 15 or so beautiful young women; some of the most beautiful women I have ever seen.

The head of the Mafia told Kim to tell me, "Go ahead. Pick whichever one you want."

These most gorgeous women all stood up on the side of the street waiting as I made my final decision. It was a whole different world than what I'd been living the last few months. I was more than happy to indulge in this unexpected delight.

The next morning, they drove me through the rice paddies and back up to my mountaintop.

The first thing I did when I got back to my post was go to my commanding officer and let him know what had happened. The

Korean Mafia wanted to pay me to divert supplies to their operations, but I knew what I wanted was to catch them.

My commanding officer said, "Well, I have to run this up the flagpole here. Nobody's ever been in this situation before."

Within a few days, I was no longer working directly for the United States Army. Instead, I was working for the CIA.

Imagine. Here I am, 19 years old, I graduated high school with a 1.8 GPA, nearly killed myself, and now I am working for the CIA.

We set everything up and made a bunch of supply runs. I was never on the trucks. Each week, we took five of my trucks with my people and went to the different supply points. We picked up gas, microwaves, refrigerators, and all kinds of stuff; all American made, owned, and paid for by the U.S. Government. They would fill up the trucks at each of the different supply points. They would then drop off the supplies wherever we were told to deliver. Everything went directly into the hands of the Korean Mafia. This continued for a couple of months.

Until one day. This day is different.

We switched the trucks out.

The trucks were filled at the supply points as usual. However, on this day after the trucks loaded with supplies and we traveled through a small village, my trucks were switched out for other trucks that were filled with military soldiers. When the trucks pulled up to the drop off point where the Korean Mafia waited, the soldiers jumped out and captured everyone in the Korean Mafia.

Everyone, except for the head of the Mafia.

All of his Lieutenants and his security were captured. The Mafia King's entire operation was shut down. Everyone was surprised that day. In less than an hour, the entire Korean Mafia was disassembled except for the head of the Mafia.

Immediately, my life was in danger! That same day, I was flown out of Korea to Japan for safety.

> *Now, here I am arriving in Japan with full military honors. A huge party is thrown in my honor. The Army awards me with the highest non-combat war medal called the Army Commendation Medal. I am a hero. I took down the Korean Mafia.*

I left Korea with many blessings. One was especially heartfelt. I found out that James, the soldier who said he had a complete background check done on me, actually lied. He made that whole story up. He conjured up the entire story of how I would never amount to anything because he was jealous of me. I didn't realize it at the time.

A Stroll Through the Japan Zoo

I remember one day when I decided to visit the Japan Zoo. Picture a tall, white soldier, wearing dog tags and eating a bag of peanuts. I towered above everyone in the crowd. I stopped to look at little caged monkeys. As I came up to the front of the cage, this one little monkey started to jump up and down and looked like it was mad. I didn't know what was wrong, but I was curious so I kept watching. I thought maybe I looked different and that upset him. Man, this little monkey kept jumping up and down while he held the bars. I got a little closer to the cage when all of a sudden...

Whomp! He took my bag of peanuts!

He was doing all that jumping around and hooting to entice me so he could get my bag of peanuts. Smart little guy!

Next, I walked down to where there was a beautiful lion. The lion paced back and forth in its big cage enclosure. When I came up to the lion, his eyes were on me. He was in his cage, but he had a large area to roam around in and as he paced, he kept his eyes on mine. I noticed the Japanese people were all moving away from me. I thought maybe they were afraid of the lion, but then realized there's no way the lion was going to get out and attack. There were bars, so there's no problem. Still, the people all kept moving away, and I couldn't understand why. The lion kept looking at me and watched intently as he paced back and forth. As I stood there watching him, his tail went up, and he ruffled his back.

He didn't look happy at all.

All of a sudden, he looked at me from the side, turned around, lifted his tail... and farted, shooting poop all over me! I literally had lion crap all over me!

The Japanese people were howling and laughing. I think the Japanese knew what was about to happen, and that's why they had ditched. They knew this lion was known for that. Of course, I didn't know; I was a stupid American GI. They thought it hilarious that I got farted on by the lion.

I remember I went into the restroom to clean myself up as best as I could. I took the bus back to the Post, and I could read the expression on the person's face who sat next to me thinking, "Oh, this GI really stinks."

Of course, I did! There was lion crap all over me!

An American Hero

I spent 13 months in Korea, which was the required amount of time there. I was in Japan for about six weeks when the U.S. started reducing our involvement in Vietnam. The U.S. General stationed in Japan, along with about 300 troops, were left to manage the entire operation. I was sent back to the United States.

Now I am a highly decorated soldier, took down the Korean Mafia, and I'm only 19 years old.

It's kind of funny, but I always liked telling the Mafia story when I was dating. I would tell them that I worked for the Korean Mafia.

My dates were all like, "Oh, my gosh, that's terrible. How could you do that and not be loyal to the United States?"

I would laugh.

Actually, I was the most loyal person to the United States. I risked my life in Korea because I wanted to do something good. The golden opportunity came to me in a chance to become a hero by taking down the Korean Mafia. I jumped at the opportunity.

CHAPTER 2

Viva Las Vegas

1971. It was an exciting time for me. I attended a large high school outside of Milwaukee, Wisconsin. I was a partier and I had so much fun. I was part of this club called the UniBoys or UB for short. "Uni" was short for Universal Beer that was brewed in a local suburb of Milwaukee in Oshkosh, Wisconsin. The UniBoys and I would party all the time. All the time.

I didn't focus on my grades at all.

I was having fun beyond my wildest imagination. I was on the student council, prom court, and pretty well known. I had the most beautiful girlfriend in the entire school; Jennifer was stunning. I was like a kid in a candy store with a wad of cash, and I made the most of it by having the best time I could.

Contrasting Experiences

The first time I was sick in high school, my father wrote an excuse note for me to give to the Principal. Before I handed it in, I took the note my father had written and destroyed it. I rewrote the note in my own handwriting. My father had a stamp of his signature, so I used his stamp. That became the legitimate note.

That way, when the Principal compared the notes to the first note, they all would match.

I missed school as much as half of the time. I wrote notes saying things like, "He has a serious illness. We aren't sure how long he is going to make it..." I was not in school much at all. I had too many fun things to do!

I signed the notes, forging my dad's signature, when really I was out water skiing on Rock River with the family boat, going up to our farm in the middle of Wisconsin, or having fun, wild parties at my parents' home while they were gone on the weekends.

Despite all the fun I am having, this is also a time when there are many "contrasts" in my life. What I call contrasts are what most people refer to as bad times. I simply see experiences as a contrast between what I do want and what I don't want. Contrast helps me clearly define what I do want. It's all good so there really isn't any bad.

Here I am a senior in high school. I have everything that I want. I have all this joy. And I have contrasts...

I drove around in a brand new blue Camaro. That was a hot car. It was actually my mother's. When my mom and dad would leave on the weekends, they took my dad's station wagon. I had this beautiful, hot Camaro to drive around.

This one day, Jennifer called me from a friend's house, so I hopped in the car. I thought I could do and have everything that I wanted, which is true; but I wasn't paying attention to the laws on earth. I drove on this back road in the city of Wauwatosa on my way to see Jennifer at 75 miles an hour.

The speed limit was 25.

About three blocks in front of me, I saw a car stop, and then pull right out in front of me to cross the road. I was going too fast. I knew that I wouldn't survive if I was in the car when it crashed. (This was one of those moments when I knew I was protected. I was being called to open the door.) I put my hand on the handle and slammed on my brakes. I hit the guy. Ran right into him. On impact, the door opened, and I was thrown from the car.

Immediately the Camaro flipped over, and I was on my hands and knees holding up the car. The car was on my back, and I was literally holding it up. It was the adrenalin pushing through. I screamed for help.

Jennifer heard the collision. She was eight blocks away, and figured it was probably me because I was the wildest guy, going fast all the time in my hot Camaro.

My car was totaled. All four tires blown.

Miraculously, I was alive and there weren't any serious injuries to any other people. My entire back was scraped and my knees were swollen and sprained. I don't remember how they even got the car off of me.

Teen-age Pregnancy

About six weeks later, I found out that Jennifer was pregnant. At my parents' cottage we would make love on this large brass bed. That is where it happened. We had made love there many times, but this one time, I knew instantly she was pregnant. I just knew.

I have all these contrasts.

The first is my car accident, and then when Jennifer becomes pregnant, and finally, I am about to graduate with a 1.8 GPA out of 4.0. My life is a mess.

A few days later, Jennifer flew out to be with her mother who lived in Las Vegas, Nevada. When I told Jennifer's dad about the situation, of course he threatened to kill me. I decided that I would fly out to Las Vegas so that Jennifer and I could decide what we were going to do. This was right before high school graduation.

Jennifer's mother was best friends with Ann Otis. Ann Otis was the heir to Otis Elevator and was part owner in many casinos at that time. I arrived in Las Vegas, only 17 years old, and was picked up in a limo by Ann Otis, Jennifer, and her mother.

Because of Ann, we spent the week watching amazing shows and going behind stage to meet the actors. Again, I lived a life of contrast, where everything was wonderful on the outside, but at the same time, I was faced with needing to decide what to do with my already messed-up life.

I hadn't even graduated yet, had no education per se, and no job experience. I had nothing.

Ann let me know that when I turned 18, which was only a month away, that I could be a casino dealer and kind of work my way up in the casino world. I wasn't sure I wanted to do that, but I appreciated the offer.

I wasn't sure if Jennifer was in love with me or with my fame, my popularity, my good looks, and all the good stuff in my life.

Really, I was afraid that Jennifer would become like her mother.

Jennifer's mother had been married and divorced seven times. She went from one marriage to the next. I was afraid that Jennifer might be the same way. What if her mother married an attorney next? That attorney would handle a divorce between Jennifer and myself, and Jennifer would get all the money and an exit out of our marriage.

Both my dad and Jennifer's dad had given me several hundred dollars to fly out to Las Vegas and still have money to get back home. When I arrived in Las Vegas, I gave Jennifer's mother all the money I had.

At that time, abortion was legal in California; however, it would cost thousands of dollars. Jennifer, her mother, and I made the decision that Jennifer would go to California and have an abortion.

After our decision, Jennifer's mom kicked me out of the house. Not only did she kick me out of the house, she wouldn't give me back the money. So there I was in Las Vegas, in the middle of the desert, not knowing anybody, no phone, no nothing, not a penny on me, bum leg from my accident, and nowhere to go.

I started to hitchhike when I remembered where Ann Otis lived. I went to Ann's gated home, a big beautiful home with a garden. I walked up to the gate as a long-haired hippie; a big guy with a long beard and long hair. I told the guard that I would like to speak with Ann Otis.

He said, "Nobody is allowed in. She doesn't want any visitors today."

I said, "Well, my name is Hank Seitz."

The guard said, "What? What's your name again?"

I said, "I'm Hank Seitz."

Then he said, "Oh my God, there's only one person that Ann is going to allow in today. Are you sure you're Hank Seitz?"

I had to show him my ID. I was a hippie walking up to the gate with nothing but the clothes on my back. He didn't want to believe that I was the Hank Seitz that Ann was willing to allow in that day.

Sure enough, she let me in. She had a plane ticket home for me. She knew exactly what was going on. Ann actually took me to the airport and escorted me onto the plane. Back then, there weren't all the regulations that there are now. She had a lot of pull and basically warmed everything up for me. So, back home I went.

It's the Army Life for Me

I graduated the next week with a whopping 1.8 GPA, still limping along from my car accident.

I thought, what in the hell am I going to do? I was depressed about the abortion and feeling guilt over the death of my child. My father wanted me to go to a private rich boy's school in Wisconsin. I wanted to go to school in Oshkosh, Wisconsin, which was a party town, but he wasn't willing to pay for that. We were at an impasse.

My dad was disappointed in me.

After giving me an amazing childhood, I had barely graduated high school, totaled my car, and gotten a girl pregnant.

I decided to enlist. The Vietnam War was in full swing. My dad drove me to the Army Enlistment Office in Milwaukee. Since I was about a month away from being 18 years old, my dad had to sign a release before I could join. He did that for me.

I was now a soldier in the United States Army.

It is the early 70s and I am the last guy in the world anybody would consider likely to enlist in the military. I am a big proponent of more freedom and peace and the peace symbol. However, I also have a strong loyalty to the United States given my family's military heritage. My father was 19 when he set his sights on training to become a pilot for World War II. I find me enlisting in the Army kind of ironic.

I was torn. On one hand, I thought, "Oh my gosh, what am I doing? Who on earth would do that? Join the military? During a war?" On the other hand, I didn't know any other option. I didn't want go to my dad's private school. I didn't want to be under his rule anymore. I wanted to get away from that. I wanted more freedom.

The military was the biggest and best choice that I knew I could make.

I had debts to pay—I had to pay Jennifer's parents back since they had paid for her abortion. I wanted to repay that debt. As I reflect, it was my way to release myself from the guilt I was feeling. The military was the place I could go right away to start making money. I didn't need any extra money. I used the dorms and chow hall to sleep and eat. Every penny that I earned went to Ann Otis to pay for the airplane ticket, then to my dad and Jennifer's dad. It took me about two years of my full salary to do that.

After I enlisted, I had a few days to say goodbye to my friends and have a great party. I had to go through basic training first, which was in Fort Knox, Kentucky. My first day of basic training was on my 18th birthday.

What a way to celebrate my birthday.

I Want to Experience War

I wanted to experience war but I didn't want to die in it. Since I was a recruit, I could choose my occupation. I decided I wanted to be a Supply Sergeant. After basic training, I then went to Virginia for my training in supply. I actually ended up in missile supply.

To forget about the abortion and the turmoil in my life, I gave training everything I had. I was a sharpshooter and got promoted fast. I had letters of recommendation for a bunch of different awards, one of them being the top graduate in my class. I dedicated myself. Physically, I was an amazing medalist. I wanted to show them I was ready to go. I was making up for my past.

At missile supply training I graduated with honors. Then I went back home to Milwaukee for a week before I flew to Washington state. At that time, no matter what your branch of the military, you were flown to Washington first. In Washington I received my orders to Vietnam and gear. There was special Vietnam gear with camouflage and everything.

It was about three days before I was scheduled to leave for Vietnam when President Nixon called back the troops. At that moment, no other troops were to be sent to Vietnam. They changed my orders from Vietnam to South Korea.

I knew absolutely nothing about Korea.

CHAPTER 3

The Power to Create Reality

This is how I became stationed on top of a mountain in the middle of nowhere.

I was given access to five different supply points to include Seoul, but I was literally stuck up on top of this mountain. To get to any location, I had to drive through miles of rice paddies.

I was desperate. I felt alone, with an immense amount of guilt, worthlessness, and the feeling of being disempowered. However, even with a gun to my head, there was still something there. I had all of this negativity and guilt; but yet there it was, something calling my soul. There was something more I could sense. Something else that most would call God, that I call God, calling me from a distance.

Then, I actually heard a small "voice."

Ever so barely, I could attach to the connection that we all have.

None of us are able to cut off that connection completely, but sometimes we make it as thin as a thread. That's where I was. I was hanging onto my life by a thread because I kept thinking about the things that I didn't want. I kept thinking of the things that hadn't worked out. I kept thinking of all my mistakes.

In that moment of despair with the gun to my head, I realized that when we have faith and believe, then we're never alone. There never was anything to feel guilty or bad about, because there was always a solution, an answer. There was an understanding that superseded my own mental capacity to understand that everything that happened, happened for my betterment, for my own good. For Jennifer's good, too.

I had gotten to a low point in my life, possibly the lowest ever. This understanding helped me to rebound, to bounce up and change direction.

Draw on the Power of Contrast to Sink Deep Roots

Imagine that each of our lives is a tree. We each have roots that build on the contrast of the things we don't like. The deeper the roots are, the higher our trees can grow.

That low point in my life allowed me to build deep roots.

My roots were: sadness, guilt, desperation, and feeling alone. Those were the roots I used to build the foundation for my magnificent tree, to make the gorgeous branches of life and growth that we each have in store for us.

> *To grow the roots deep down to anchor myself, I have life experiences that create strength within. I need those deep roots. It is those deep roots that I use to develop the magnificent tree that I am now. I need those deep roots to stand tall and unwavering in my belief each and every day.*
>
> *No wind or storm can ever blow me over.*
>
> *I have the deep roots that I have built this beautiful tree on. It is the essence of me.*

That night, with the gun to my head, the hammer pulled back, and my finger on the trigger, something called to me. There was an awareness of something greater than my physical body, greater than my own mind. There was something that called me back to life.

From that moment on, I began a journey of happiness, joy, and prosperity.

…a journey focused more on the things that I wanted.

…a journey filled with more enlightenment.

I have the deepest connection with the Spirit of God, and I attribute it to all my life experiences. Returning from this low, low time is one of the key life experiences that helps me develop this deep and meaningful relationship.

I call it a crystal clarity.

Crystal Clarity is that moment when I know that I am never alone. My inner being is always there, despite whatever circumstances or situations are happening in the world. I stand tall because I am in a state of crystal clarity.

It was as if I'd rejected my thoughts, my father's thoughts, and Jennifer's father's thoughts. Instead, I surrendered to the Higher Being that I was destined to be.

Through the years, that experience helped me to recognize that I could overcome any circumstance, event, or experience. As I grew, so did the feeling of "all is well." It was my first step. I thought, "Wow! All is well no matter what is going on in my life."

And I realize another truth. I take the second step. I recognize that we are all creators of our lives. I create my life.

We are all creators, but not all of us are deliberate creators. Most of us create by happenstance. We think a force outside of us is creating our life, and we have to take what comes to us.

This is not true.

I recognized in my "lowest of the low" moment that I could become a deliberate creator and create my experience the way that I wanted it. I saw that "contrast" gave me insight to what I wanted. I needed to feel the opposite of the disempowerment I was experiencing. I realized that I could go to the highest level of opposite feeling, and that was empowerment.

Immediately, I felt the highest level of freedom!

I felt the empowerment, freedom, and love.

Without my situation, I would not have discovered that freedom. I know that there are many paths to enlightenment, but this was my path to enlightenment. That was step one for me, to get down so excruciatingly low. Others don't have to go that low, but for me, I went to the bottom.

I face the lowest of lows and stand today as "The Happiest Man in the World!"

The contrast was why I met the Korean Mafia with such power. Did I have faith when I was going to meet the Korean Mafia? You bet I did! I knew it was going to go well.

Some people might have asked, "What's going to happen next?"

For me, from that moment on, I *knew* what would happen next... something wonderful. That's what was going to happen next, something wonderful! I realized that I could create my future by seeing my future first. I realized that something wonderful would always be right there, no matter what!

I have the knowledge that makes it possible to have something wonderful happen because I create my own experience.

At the time I don't get it completely. But when I do, it brings me to the point of understanding. I am connected with my inner being, called God. When I am connected, then all is well. I always know that something wonderful for me is right around the corner.

The night that I was at the supply point with the gun to my head, I recognized the voice that said, "All is well." I understood that I needed to think with God, with my Source, and start looking for the goodness that was all around me.

From 1.8 to 4.0

After Japan, they stationed me at Fort Sill, Oklahoma for the remainder of my enlistment. It was almost a year. I was out of the CIA and back in the Army again.

Here I am with these incredible life experiences that show me I can do anything, be anything.

No longer am I the kid with a 1.8 GPA who barely got out of high school with a diploma. Now, I'm a military hero with the Military Commendation Medal.

I did things in my first three years of service that most people would never dream of doing in a lifetime. I was promoted quickly and worked with the CIA to bring down the Korean Mafia. That was an amazing thing to do, and that is what fueled my determination to go to college.

I went to the University of Wisconsin, Madison. Even though I started my first semester on probation, I reversed the experience of getting bad grades in high school and ended up getting straight A's in college. I was on the Dean's List every semester. I graduated with a 4.0 GPA. It was my life experience that helped me to realize that I could do whatever the hell I wanted to do.

What I did was dedicate myself to school. Instead of skipping out to have a good time as I had in high school, I dedicated myself to have a good time while getting good grades. I went to every class, got every assignment complete on time, and pulled straight A's.

This goes to show you that no matter how other people judge you, in grades or whatever it is; it doesn't matter. All of us can set our minds to whatever we want and achieve our goals. Each of us has the opportunity for a "redo" every single moment of our lives.

> *Reality doesn't exist in our world. Yes, this physical world is our reality. Where reality is created, however, is in dreams and our imagination. I stay in tune with my dreams and aspirations. The more in tune I am, the more I create in the physical world.*
>
> *People tell me, and have told me for most of my life, "Why don't you face reality?"*
>
> *I say, "No, I'm not going to face reality, I create reality."*
>
> *This is a motto that I use regularly. I, and each one of us, has the power to create reality. I create reality through my imagination, through my dreams.*

Think about what is going on right now. Think about what will be, and how do you want it to be? Have that in mind and be patient. Know that it's coming. The Universe is conjuring it up; the perfect lighted path for you and all of your dreams.

If you start saying to yourself, "Oh, that probably won't happen." Then you subconsciously ask for that, and so you shall receive. That's what you get, "it's not going to happen." You'll never face whatever reality that you're up against.

In fact, don't face it. Don't face reality. Start to create your future reality instead. If you don't like your current reality, start creating what you do want.

I did want something different from my previous reality so I was determined in the military to be the best, and I was. I have the medals and promotions to prove it. I took down the Korean Mafia. I did amazing things.

From there, I was determined that I would get through college, go to a top ranked school, and be hired by a corporation in America. After graduation, I was hired by Procter and Gamble, one of the top corporations in the world.

I did it. I still do it. And you can do it, too.

One of the best things that came to me while I was up on the mountain, was that I gained access to those five supply points, the trucks, and Seoul Air Force Base, which had everything imaginable: blankets, fuel, refrigerators, microwaves. Of course when I was approached by the Korean Mafia, I immediately thought this was suspicious. Then, I came from a place of expecting a great opportunity. I figured, you know what? I'm going to play along with this.

I lightened up and decided that I would roll with whatever life gave me. I started to think about what I wanted, a new opportunity to be happy. I knew I could make it through this, and I knew that I had the opportunity I was looking for.

I did things on my side and started to bring power and love and attraction to what I was thinking.

You can do it, too. You can bring the power, love and attraction to what you're thinking about next. Put it all on your side of the table and begin to build on that.

Chapter 4

Prepare for Anything

The greatest impact on my life as a child was my dominant father. He was a disciplinarian, always rough and tough. The "you've got to go do what I mean" type of father.

He was an only child growing up and probably lonely. After he graduated high school, World War II was happening. Instead of getting recruited, he decided to enlist in the Air Force. They had these 90-day wonders where you could become a pilot in 90 days. My father was so obstinate that everything he did was right. Therefore, joining the Air Force was the right and smart thing to do, regardless if it really was.

Usually wherever the crowd was going, my father was walking in the other direction. Case in point, he was not going to just enlist, but he was going to be a pilot. He became a bomber pilot and a Captain.

When I was a boy, he shared with me a story about flying over Germany the fateful day he was shot down. Normally, they flew pretty high, so the guns or cannons being shot up at the plane couldn't reach that high. During this one flyover, the Germans kept shooting up in the air, and sometimes they got lucky.

My father had about 12 people in his plane: the gunners, the bombardiers, co-pilot, and a navigator. As the plane was going down, everybody parachuted out. He was the last one out of the plane; the pilot is always the last to jump out.

As he was drifting down in his parachute, he could see a MiG German fighter with machine guns on both wings coming straight towards him. My dad was helpless. He waved. You know, kind of like, "Hello." My father caught the eye of the pilot and made a kind of "mankind-to-mankind, please don't shoot me" plea. The German pilot was that close.

The German pilot didn't wave back. Instead, he stared him down, circled around, and came right back toward my dad. My father knew the German was going to open up those machine guns, and he would be history.

All of a sudden, my father heard behind him, "All is well."

It startled him, he looked behind him as he thought maybe somebody had jumped out after him. He looked behind, but nobody was there.

He heard it again, "All is well."

He was shaking, holding onto the cords, as he was floating down. He was totally helpless. He thought somebody must have parachuted out after him. Again, he turned and looked behind, but he didn't see anyone.

He was watching the German MiG coming right toward him again, and he knew this would be the last moment that he would ever have when out of the clouds came the American machine gunners, and they got into a dogfight. The German took off, and the Americans shot down the German MiG. My father landed safely.

Those exact words I heard in Korea, "All is well," resonated with my father, too.

Of course, my father landed on German soil. As the farmers were shooting at him, he got hit in the knee. He was captured and placed in a German prison camp throughout the winter. No one in the prison camp ever knew when they woke up in the morning if they were going to have food, if they were going to be shot, or if they would even be alive by the time the sun set.

It was a traumatic time for my father. He was a kid, only 19 years old. It was similar to my experience in Korea when I worked with the Korean Mafia. The similarities that he and I share are interesting.

General Patton eventually came in with our troops and freed him. He was in prison for almost a year, and that experience emotionally and psychologically played with him the rest of his life.

He arrived back home to Wisconsin a war hero.

A Tough Love Upbringing

As a big war hero, my father was well respected and determined to marry the most beautiful woman in Milwaukee, and he did—a model named Shirleen who was my mother. Together, my parents had four sons. (I am the third oldest.)

My father also was determined to bring his sons up and show us how tremendously tough life can be. He realized, when he was in the German prison camp at a young age that he had not been prepared to take the trauma that had happened to him there; the bugs, the hunger, and the not knowing if he was going to be shot.

Since he felt he couldn't handle being a POW at 19 and because in his mind, he loved us so much, he would prepare us for whatever came our way. He never showed us love per se, but what he did to us was definitely out of love for us.

In our two-story home, I could look out the window and see the garage which was in the backyard. I hated that moment when my father drove up after his work day and walked into the house. I shook, not knowing if I had done anything wrong that I might be in trouble for. He was tough and abusive.

Some of the experiences during my upbringing were unnerving. One time, my two older brothers and I were riding in a car with our dad. I was maybe five years old.

We were on a dirt road, and he took us up to the top where there was only the dirt road and then forest on both sides. He dropped the three of us off, and he sped off. Apparently, we must have done something wrong. I didn't know what it was. He left us there, in the middle of nowhere.

The fear overwhelmed me, you know; no dad, no shelter, no food, no nothing. He left us out there. My brothers who are four and five years older than I am, had been fairly used to him doing this. I remember one other time when he dropped us off, my brothers laid down and said, "He'll be back."

They already had figured out that he always ended up coming back.

I'm sure Dad was thinking that he was going to leave us out in the middle of nowhere, like he had been left in Germany.

Another time, I was sitting on the couch watching TV, and I got tired. I laid down and fell asleep. Out of nowhere, my father came up shaking me and screaming in my face, "What are you doing sleeping?! Get up, you lazy kid!"

He wanted to teach me how to become a man. What he did was scare the living hell out of me.

> *I've been told by a behavioral psychologist that there's nothing worse that can happen to you when you are asleep. You have no protective defenses up, no barrier of defense. You go from this tender loving, majestic sleep, to immediately being shaken awake in terror. It literally sends these terror emotions straight into your cells, into your DNA. It changes you and puts fear into you.*

I lived in this circumstance of fear all the time.
I never knew what to expect.

> *It is because of these abusive experiences I endured that I want to make sure you understand that everything we think is bad (contrast) actually helps us birth wonderful ideas in our future.*

> *For example, I became a wonderful father to my children and showed them unconditional love because of what my father could not show me.*

Not only was my father abusive, but so, too, were my two older brothers who took great pride in tormenting me. Remember, they were four and five years old when I came into the picture. My brothers are only 10 months apart, and they had already been hanging out together having fun for four years. From the moment I was born, I was a problem for them.

They resented me because now I was goofing up things. They had to babysit me. They didn't like that because they would rather have gone out to play.

So the Abused Become the Abusers

The earliest time I remember their abuse is when I first tried to walk. I was up on a table kind of wobbling. I was crawling up the table and feeling so proud that I had pulled myself up from that table, and I was starting to take a couple of steps. I was so happy. Then, from out of nowhere with no warning, I was pushed. It was one of my brothers who pushed me down.

From the time I was out of the womb, they would continue to get any small triumph they could over me. I later discovered that my mother would say in front of my brothers that I was the best looking son. This created a tremendous amount of animosity and jealousy.

I was the best looking.

I was the most charming.

That added to the fuel.

I have a notion based on later years with my father about that. I don't think he wanted to ever say it, but I think he considered me his favorite son, too. So, he wanted to lay the hammer on me even worse because of that. He wanted to make sure that I could protect myself and that I could stand up against anything. I think because my dad perceived that I had life easier than my brothers, he felt he had a responsibility to be even harder, rougher, and tougher on me. I was born into this charmed life and looking good.

Now, my brothers on the other hand, were driven by jealousy.

They discovered how fun it was to torture me.

It was in the summer and on the grass where they pinned me down while they dug their knees into my arms so I couldn't get away. They would do what they called "Chinese torture." So, while I was in great pain with their knees dug into my biceps, they would hold my head and stick grass into my nose.

I was helpless.

It would kind of tickle, but I was so mad.

I would try with all my might to get out of there. No matter how hard I tried, I couldn't get away. I was pinned down, enslaved. Totally disempowered. I would keep trying with all my might to get out of this situation, but I had to give up. There was nothing worse for me than to have to give up.

They would do horrendous things. And, it became one thing on top of another, adding to the abuse of my father.

When my parents weren't around, I was tortured and physically hurt by them. They would make me do errands for them. I had to clean the house or do whatever errands they were supposed to do. I had to do it all. So, I was a slave to them. I was abused both physically and mentally by them.

They made my life a living hell.

Mother earth has given me these deep roots. Now, as I stand as a solid, strong, healthy tree, the tree of life, all is well. Not only do I not need to be protected anymore, there's nothing to be protected from. There is only wellbeing that flows into this life. I think about how I am free and that I want even more and more of it. All of that contentious upbringing is a blessing for me.

CHAPTER 5

If It Moves, Kill It

Father was a hunter. My father had every imaginable place in Wisconsin to go kill animals. He bought a farm, not to do farming on it, but for hunting. There were a lot of whitetail deer there. Whitetails are beautiful, majestic animals. The farm was loaded with them. That area has one of the greatest populations of whitetail deer per square mile.

I was brought up to hunt. The way we would hunt was to get eight hunters on the one side of the forest. They would start walking the forest back and forth scaring up all the deer. There would be shooters sitting on the other side of the forest. As the walkers would scare up the deer, the hunters on the other side would shoot them. BOOM!

You could shoot as many deer as you wanted if they were bucks. That was legal.

However, we shot fawns, does, bucks; it didn't matter. Most of the things that my father, my brothers, and I did when I was a child were illegal. It didn't matter if it was deer hunting season or not. We went out there whenever we wanted to shoot deer.

That Bird Isn't Going to Live

I was brought up in a world where you shot everything that moved. If there were blackbirds on the telephone wire, you shot them dead. If there was a goose or duck flying through the air, you shot it. If there was a deer running by, you shot it. If there was a squirrel, you shot it. I mean literally, anything that moved, you shot it.

I didn't know any differently.

In Rock River, Wisconsin, at our cottage, I had wounded a bird that was sitting on a telephone wire. I shot it, and it fell down and was making sounds like it was in pain. For the first time, I realized what I was doing. I didn't want that bird dead, so I decided I was going to take care of it.

My father was gone that day working in the city. So the whole day, I made a little box as a nest for the bird. I gave it worms. I did everything I could to help this bird get better. I was proud of my handiwork.

My father came back from the city, and said, "What are you doing?"

I said, "Well, I'm healing this bird."

He walked up, and said, "That bird isn't going to live."

He grabbed the bird and pulled the head right off.

I was horrified. I was torn apart emotionally. What cruelty to an animal! Why? I couldn't put it into words at the time. It was a terrible feeling to witness death. It was a part of growing up.

> *I am only four or five years old. I have this tenderness, and I believe we're all born as tender, angelic beings. Then our experiences harden us up. I am unwilling to harden up. I still have feelings for the animals.*

We had a cottage on Silver Lake. My dad had gone back into town. He owned his own CPA firm and eventually a construction company. He left us there alone, giving my brothers more opportunity to abuse me. My brothers knew that I was sensitive to what we would call today, animal cruelty.

Because of that, they held me hostage while they went and got turtles that were about eight to 10 inches in diameter. (There were a lot of turtles there.) They set a turtle down in front of me, had this big axe, and cut that turtle right in half. They would laugh, while I would be crying, "Don't do it. Please, don't do it."

Then it got worse.

Another time, we were at this one farm we owned. And again, my dad was not around, so my brothers could be naughty. Of course, they were being kids and doing what they had been taught, but they were cruel kids.

It was at night, and we had a bonfire by this pond. My brothers caught a cat and put him in a burlap bag. Then, they wrapped a big heavy rope around the bag and extended the rope about 10 feet. They got a post, pounded the post into the ground, and tied the other end of the rope from the bag to the post. They poured gasoline on the burlap bag with this cat in it, and they lit it up.

They lit the cat on fire.

It was awful. Truly awful.

I vividly remember this poor cat running in circles around this pole. It started to get burned.

The smell was acrid. The cat screamed horrifically in agony.

My brothers laughed.

They laughed and said, "Gee, look at that," totally pleased with their handiwork.

I was in utter terror.

I watched this cat running wildly, screeching as it burned to death. They ran to get the other end of the post and swing it around. They tied a rock around it and threw it into the lake.

Down went the rock. Down went the burning burlap bag and the cat to its death.

They were cruel and abusive.

In my brothers' case, they had a lot of anger. The way my father was so suppressive to them, they needed an out, they needed an escape. They were abused, so they wanted to abuse.

> *If parents abuse, typically, their kids end up being abusers as well. I think at the bottom, it is that you want to strike out over the abuse and you strike out in the same way, the same behavior on someone or something else. It is a way of having control.*

Paul, my youngest brother, was an "accident." He was born five years after me, creating even more upset in our already upset life.

My brothers were older, like 10 and 11 at that time. They were pretty much out of the picture. I was at home doing other activities. They were more out on their own.

My youngest brother didn't get as much abuse from them, but probably got a little from me. We had bunk beds. I was on the top bunk, and he kept kicking it when we would go to sleep. One night, I got ticked off, and I grabbed him by the hair and held him there. He had to half stand up. I was starting to be abusive to him, but I wasn't abusive to animals.

Unfortunately, Paul also was under the uncompromising command of my father. He turned out much like my father and today, treats his children rough and tough; whereas, I went to the opposite end and showed unconditional love to my children. Paul grew up to be most like my dad. He even looks like dad.

Coming from a Place of Fear and Anger

When I was a General Manager with Procter and Gamble, I had a lot of deep anger and a fear within me. I went to a psychologist, and it was helpful.

It was then that I realized that my dad and my brothers were abusive to me. I didn't know that. I thought how I was raised was normal. Once my brothers were out of high school and going to college, they were out of my life. Whereas my father, throughout my college years; was still there: always the dictator with abusive towards me.

I worked on forgiveness and tried to understand my brothers. I shared with my mother what I was doing and what they had done to me while Father and she were away. She went and shared it with my two older brothers by saying, "How could you torture Hank and put grass in his nose?"

They didn't like hearing any of that stuff. The next time I saw them, we were taking a family picture and my one brother grabbed a little piece of grass. He was four feet away from me and threated to stick the grass up my nose.

I immediately wanted to jump out and pound on him. At the time I could have easily done it, too. I was fit. I had been in the Army. They were no longer the older, bigger brothers.

I didn't do anything. The fear was gone.

The insurance industry invested millions of dollars to figure out that the number one reason for death in the United States, heart disease, comes from stress. They started looking at stress and found it comes from fear. But you know what? They found that over 90% of the things we fear never even happen to us.

This is huge!

Think of how many things you are worried about that will never happen! We start thinking about what we are worried about, and 10% of the fear that comes true is all because we were thinking about it. We created it in our own mind.

With that, my fear was gone.

The anger hung around longer. I remember my brother's threat with the grass really stirred me.

They thought it was a big joke which pissed me off even more.

CHAPTER 6

German Bayonet Knife

By the time I was in fifth grade, I was so terrified of my father and brothers and so exhausted from living on the edge, that I went up to the little office my father had with one intention, and one intention only. In the closet, my father had a German bayonet from World War II hanging on the wall. It was his prized possession. He was so proud of that bayonet, and that he was a military hero.

My hands shook, my heart raced as I reached up and took the knife. I walked back to my father's desk and steadied myself. I couldn't take it anymore. I took the knife in both of my hands and turned it towards my chest. I held the point left of my breastbone, knowing this was the quickest and easiest way to penetrate my heart.

I was going to push with all my might.

I was going to shove that knife right into my heart and end the terror, the pain, the disconnection, and the absolute horror that I was living. As I was getting up the gumption to shove it into my heart, there was something that wouldn't let me do it. Something called me, told me, this wasn't what I wanted.

I was beside myself. I released the knife and broke down in tears. Not tears of pain, but tears of awe. Tears of relief. I realized there was a blessing in all this experience of pain. There was something more than my experience of pain. I realized that I needed to get through this. Something helped me, and would help me to overcome this and go up to the summit.

> *In an instant, I went from pain, terror, tears, and near suicidal death, to enlightenment. I realized, "Oh my God, there's something more here for me. I'm not alone."*

I love that.

> *Throughout my life, I've embraced the moments where I have been so clear knowing there is something more. It has always been like something or someone talking to me; something there protecting me, keeping me safe and sound.*

That was my first experience of near suicide.

The second one as you know, was in Korea with the gun to my head. Both provided clarity and enlightenment in their own unique way.

I know my father's intention was to make me strong. I think he believed until the day that he transitioned (passed away as people say) that he was right in how he raised and brought his boys up. And, maybe so.

> *All four of us brothers are relatively happy and successful. Who knows who we could have been, or who we could have not been. What he gave me was a lot of contrasts and understanding of what I didn't want. And, contrast, showing us what we don't want, can be a strong driving force to create what we do want.*

> *Twenty years later, I have three sons of my own.*

> *I know from experience what I am not. I am not like my dad. First off, I have a strong will to show unconditional love to my*

children and let them know that they have the power to be, do, and have everything that they want.

For those of us who have children, you know that your children are precious to you. You want to do everything and anything for them. Without those experiences with my father, I don't think I would be so determined to be a good, unconditionally loving, and encouraging father to my sons. Now, I look back on it as a blessing. Everything that I went through was a blessing. My life today is a beautiful example of what a blessing that was.

Empowerment and Freedom

One day, my father called me into his office. I stood at his desk. (He had built an extension for his office on our home.) My brother, John, stood beside me, watching, and he had a good angle on all of it.

My dad was yelling at me because I had gotten a bad grade. I had gotten a "C" in some course. Rather than be afraid, I decided I would stare him down. This time, I was not going to yell or cry. He recognized my resistance immediately, and I could see that he was going to do anything he could to break my spirit and break me down.

He wanted to disempower me.

By my determination he recognized that he no longer had power with his words over me. He decided to resort to physical power; so he hit me square in the eye. My head snapped back with the force.

I didn't give a shit. I straightened my head right back up, and I kept staring him down, saying to him in my silent disgust, "You fucking son of a bitch."

I was tough. I squared my shoulders and my body moved forward as if to say, "Go ahead, you can hit me again. You can do whatever you want, but you're not getting to me. I'm not going to be impacted by you. I'm going to create the order of my life the way that I want it to go."

As I did that, my brother looked at me in pure awe. Later he shared with me, "I can't believe you just stood there."

My father saw my eye starting to swell. I had a big black and blue welt where my father had hit me. Once my father realized this, he said to me, "Now don't you be going to school and telling everybody that I hit you. Don't tell your teachers or anyone. Tell them you fell. You understand kid?"

I thought to myself, "I can't wait to get to school and tell all of my teachers and friends. I'm going to tell everybody that my father hit me!" And I did. I told everyone.

Why? Because I'm in the 6th grade, and I'm finally taking my power back and starting to recognize who I am. A year before when I had the German bayonet knife at my heart; that was the breaking point where I said to myself, "You know I'm going to get through this, help me."

All of us need to be patient and to know that what we ask for is coming. We typically want instant gratification. Resist impatience. Believe and trust that what you ask for is coming to you. It took a year after hitting that low point with the bayonet knife for me to gain the strength to stand up to my father.

Believe and trust and have patience. Don't dwell on time. If you look at how many months, weeks, days, minutes, or seconds it takes, you'll go wild. You'll say to yourself, "Hey, there's nothing happening, nobody is helping me."

The Universe is conspiring to bring everything to you when you allow it. I knew there was something there that was backing me, something there that was not only supporting me but guiding me into what I wanted. At the time, I wanted to be empowered. I wanted to be away from my father, no longer to be under this wrath. I achieved that.

I also came to understand that my brothers were kids. They just wanted to play. We are all born to expect joy in this life, and we expect to have our dreams come true. But as we grow up, people start telling us what to believe; they tell us their beliefs and expect we will believe the same. We experience circumstances and situations that take us from that expectation of joy.

That calling of mine, and for all of us, is the calling of freedom. This calling of more freedom, more empowerment, the calling of love, of tenderness, of kindness; that's our calling.

However, if we are abused, we then have a tendency to be the same way unless we can step back from it and realize what the real situation is. Much of the abuse I went through as a child had good intentions behind it. My father had good intentions to show me how rough and tough life is. My brothers had good intentions, they wanted to go play.

My childhood took me to the point of wanting to commit suicide because of the abuse from both my father and my brothers. It was also my childhood that took me away from that low place. I came, even as a child, to where I did not want to be disempowered; I did not want a lack of freedom; and I didn't want to be abused. I started to create the life that I wanted. As became true later in life that low point bore deep roots for me.

CHAPTER 7

Oh to Be Thirteen

Being 13 years old was really a time for me to recognize that I could start creating my life the way that I wanted, that I had the power.

I've shared a lot about the tragedies (what I call the contrast) of the things that I didn't want and how I used those experiences to uplift me and take me to a whole new place of understanding and becoming everything that I want to be while I'm here in this physical body in this time/space reality.

During most of my childhood, I believed that I was not the creator of my experience, and I thought that others could overcome me. I shot a fawn when I was only 11 years old. I looked at the white dots on his small back and shot it. I didn't care. I didn't think anything about it.

A couple of years later when I was 13 years old, I was walking down this trail at the farm with a .22 rifle with hollow-point bullets. When these bullets hit something, the bullet spreads out. Remember, I was taught to shoot anything that moved.

I walked through these beautiful woods. (You know the contrast. It was all this beauty and the beautiful sky, the woods, and rolling hills.) All of a sudden, I heard a movement in the woods.

I saw a deer. I brought up my rifle with the scope on it, got a bead on the head, aligned, and shot it.

That deer went down. I walked toward it. It was probably 70 yards away from me.

A .22 is not powerful. I knew I shouldn't have used it to shoot a deer. I should have used a shotgun. But I didn't care.

Suddenly, the deer made this death sound, the sound of, "I'm dying, I need help." It was the most eerie sound to hear. As I was walking up to this deer, with trees around, I saw other deer walking, some running, coming to the call.

The deer was lying in the grass, dying. It was gurgling blood in its throat and emitting this screeching sound of death. Other deer were coming towards him, even though they saw me. Deer are wary of other creatures, especially a human being nearby. Despite my being there, these deer still were coming to their comrade; to help the deer I had shot.

There were two things that I felt then. I felt the death, but I also felt the life. I felt the love and the camaraderie.

I felt the togetherness. I felt that we all were connected.

For the first time, I recognized the power and the love within nature that we're surrounded by and so often oblivious to.

Contrast. Even here. There was this high feeling of life and the desperation death feeling. I experienced both which made me realize how connected we all are.

I had made this deer suffer greatly. I wept.

I went up to the deer and put my rifle to its head and shot it to put it out of its misery. At that point, I dropped my rifle.

That was the last time I ever shot or hurt anything else, any animal or whatever, intentionally.

I never picked up a gun to shoot again. At only 13 years old, I was considered the black sheep of the family because I decided I would no longer be a hunter.

This life really is about choices, and I get to choose what I want and what I don't want. So do you.

Thirteen was one glorious time of my life. It showed me the power that I have and the ability to choose. It was the first time that I felt the true empowerment of me, not because I killed that deer, but because I decided to put down that rifle and no longer harm another animal.

I recognized that this was not for me. I was not going to be a hunter.

The impact of that was tremendous. My father was a hunter. His father was a hunter. Two of my older brothers were hunters.

I stood up and declared at 13 that I would no longer hunt and left the rifle in the woods. My brothers went out there to retrieve it, and admonished me, "How can you leave a rifle out there?"

I recognized that I had the power to start making decisions of my own despite how rough and tough my father was, and despite how my brothers were towards me.

This is the point where I realize there is something calling me and I acknowledge it.

I recognize that I am really here to experience more joy and happiness and to have a fun time.

Even at this young age I recognize that I am an explorer.

We are all explorers, and we're exploring this beautiful world of contrasts—things we don't want, and things we do want.

I decided that I was going to start focusing on the things that I do want and see how fun life was. I started exploring what I liked. I found that I was liked by other people; I was very popular.

It also was a good way to go against my father.

After that, I joined the church group which gave me an excuse to not go with my parents hunting. Because they were gone most every weekend, this also left our home in Wisconsin open for me to have wild parties as a teenager.

The Beginning of the UniBoys

I started the UniBoys to have as much fun as we possibly could. Back then we called it the gang but it was a fun gang. It wasn't like gangs now, doing drugs together. Well, we did some drugs during that time, but we did not sell them or hurt anybody else.

I was the head of this group. I loved that leadership role, and it was a fun time. We called ourselves the UB because we didn't want our parents, teachers, or society to figure out the meaning of our name. We were afraid they would try to slow us down. We loved Universal Beer!

In Wisconsin, you're raised drinking beer. My dad would say. "Okay boys, you can split a beer."

It's the mainstay in Wisconsin. Oh my, we had fun. We had a club house in the top of my parents' two-car garage. We made a big fort, and that's where we would meet. This was in the earlier years when we were about 13 years old. We went through friends. I have one friend, Johnny, who I've known since third grade.

Sleeping with Girls

I asked Johnny not too long ago, "Whatever got us connected?"

He said, "Well in 3rd grade, we were at the YMCA, and we were going to have a sleepover out at some wilderness park."

He said the leader of the YMCA asked if there were any questions. You raised your hand. There were both girls and boys, again this is in 3rd grade, and you said, "Are we going to be allowed to sleep with the girls?"

Johnny said right there he knew, "I've got to get to know this guy because he sounds like fun."

What was I thinking in 3rd grade as far as why I want to sleep with the girls? Who knows what that meant? I think it was more about kissing the girls or something.

There were about a dozen of us 7th graders in the UB, and we were definitely the most popular group in school.

I had a girl.

Her name was Sarah. We were going out, and her parents were gone. We decided to go up to her parent's master bedroom and make out. I had never ejaculated. I wasn't mature enough yet, but that was the first time that I made love to a woman.

We made love for a few minutes. I ran into the bathroom because I heard how you're supposed to run into the bathroom. I went in, and I took a pee. Of course, I didn't know what I was doing, I had this inner sense of euphoria. "Oh my God," I thought, "That was fun, it was great." I said to myself, "Hey, I'm going to have more of that."

Four or five months later, I actually did have my first ejaculation with myself in the shower. It was like, "Holy immaculate! That's what I'm talking about this is fun!"

One of the greatest misunderstandings is what sex is really about.

Sex is a couple of things.

The first is the perpetuation of our species. Sex is to help us to continue to birth new beings who want to come here, who have a desire to come here; to birth them into this world.

The second is to enhance our experience; to have more fun more often. Sex has been convoluted and misunderstood. We need only recognize that sex enhances our lives and allows us to experience more joy in our emotions, thoughts, and bodies.

We're here on this planet to enjoy ourselves. So, at 13 having sex for the first time, that was great. I realized sex is one of the beautiful, sweet fruits of life and should be enjoyed as often as I possibly could. That's what I have done all my life, but especially at this tender, naïve age of 13.

The second great misunderstanding is death.

It really is easy to understand. It's simple – there is no death. We all have eternal life.

Each of us has been here many times before. We recycle ourselves and move on to learn more lessons. Then we go into the next life whether it's here or someplace else. The reason is that we want to expand and enjoy all that is in this world.

This is beautiful. It has the perfect contrast. Everything we want, everything we don't want. We are supposed to be the explorers sifting through all of these opportunities then deciding, which one do I want? To know what I want is to understand what I don't want, hence, all the contrast.

At the time I didn't realize this but all the contrasts that I lived as a child actually helped me to birth ideas about what I did want and why I'm at this wonderful place now where I consider myself the "Happiest Man in the World."

Each of us can be the happiest person in the world. All that matters is where our focus is.

Recognize that there really is no death or consequences upon death. You simply live the way you want to live.

Chapter 8

The UniBoys

Wow. We were a wild bunch. As I've said, my father owned all kinds of different hunting places and one of them was a cottage on a river. We had a 20-foot ski boat in the shed. The UniBoys and I (with my girlfriend, Jennifer) would skip school on a beautiful spring day to go out to the river and have a great day of fun.

We had a red Mustang that could tow the boat. We pulled out the boat, took it over to the nearest bar where we could launch the boat and got ready to ski. The whole day, we had marvelous time. I was a slalom skier. Throughout the day, we would take our turns skiing and jumping the waves.

When we would get back to the cottage, Jennifer and I would make love. This was the same cottage with the big brass bed where I got her pregnant. In high school, Jennifer was the best-looking girl. She was absolutely magnificent. We had a fun time together. She had a beautiful figure and was actually a model in Vegas. She enhanced my entire experience.

We would go to the bar, too, and eat and drink. The reason we could get away with that is, we all had fake ID's. Through Jennifer's connections in Las Vegas, we had a guy that could make fake ID's for us. These were Michigan Driver's Licenses.

We didn't want Wisconsin ID's, as they couldn't duplicate

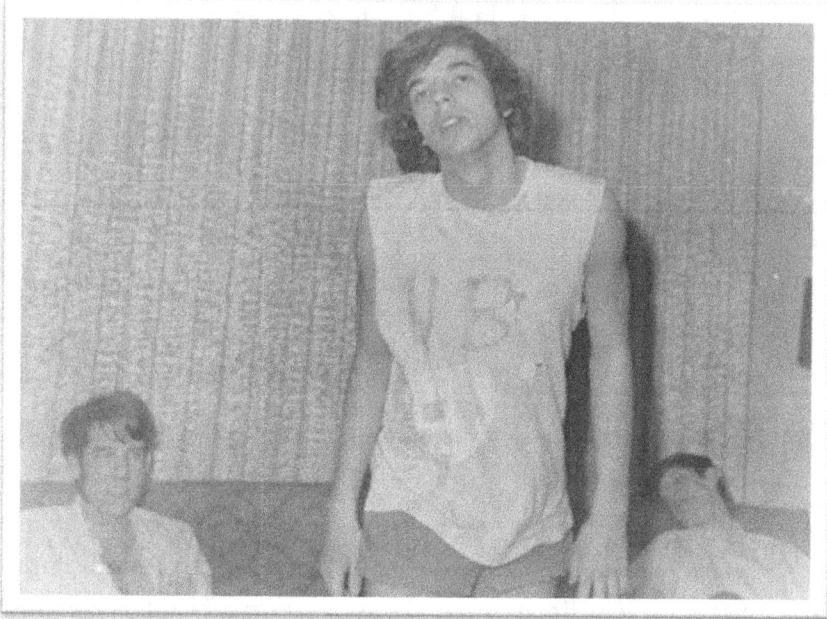

those ID's and we would get caught. So, we chose to have Michigan Driver's Licenses instead. They were good.

When the bartender put it under a red light, they could tell whether it was real. Even though it wasn't a legitimate license, it always passed. We each had fake names, too.

From Randal to Henry to Hank

I loved Henry David Thoreau. My identification card was Henry David Anderson. I figured, if I were real drunk, I would remember Anderson, and I couldn't do the "Thoreau" for a last name because most people would probably recognize Henry David Thoreau.

We were at this bar and the bartender, puts it under the red light and checks every ID then goes, "Okay what do you want?"

We were only 16 years old and were supposed to be 19 to drink. Everybody in the bar knew we were not old enough, but we had ID's. What could they do?

We start drinking. Johnny, my friend from 3rd grade was sitting next to me talking and said, "Hey Randy." (My actual given name is Randall Seitz and everybody was calling me Randy at that time.)

The bartender says, "Hey! You're not Randy. You're supposed to be Henry."

We all jumped up and ran out of the bar to our cars and took off. We made a pact that we would no longer call each other by our born Christian names, but instead we would call each other by whatever our fake ID name were. To this day, all of us call each other by our fake ID names.

For me, I went from Randy to Henry. I wasn't a Henry kind of guy and so they ended up calling me Hank. That is where Hank comes from. It has really nothing to do with my real name and has everything to do with the fake ID.

Doctor is my PhD in Mental Science. I went to school for four years to get that degree. It kind of caught on; so from the PhD to doctor, finally to Dr. Hank. That's where my name is from. But it's all kind of made up.

> *You might think that is wrong or deceitful. But, isn't everything made up? It really is, isn't it? What a realization that everything in this world is made up. All the laws are made up. Our names are made up. The term boyfriend/girlfriend is made up. What is the best car to drive is made up. It's all made up. What are you doing that you think is "real," but is really made up?*

One day we were taking the boat back to the shed after we had been on the river. We were going through these winding farm roads back to the cottage. We were going pretty fast and as we whipped around the corner, the whole boat tipped over.

My dad's boat.

There were huge scrapes on the side of the boat and it was lying on the ground. This is a huge 20-foot boat. We cannot lift it up ourselves. We have no other choice but to go to the nearby farmer and say, "Hey, you can't tell my dad about it. We tipped over the boat on the road, and we need your tractor so we can lift it back up, and put it back into the storage shed."

We got the farmer's tractor and chains and lifted the boat back up. We all became masters at fixing things. We cleaned up the boat on the side that was damaged and did a little paint job on it, then put it back in the storage room. Nobody ever noticed. The farmer didn't tell on us. We lived a charmed life and again, this is where I was feeling this freedom.

Fighting for Freedom

One of the reasons why all of us have come here is to feel more freedom and more joy. I felt freedom in that I could get away with all kinds of stuff, including missing much of my time in high school.

I was on the prom court. I was even voted president of our senior class in high school. It probably comes as no surprise that the administration could not tolerate me. They knew I was a wild guy. This is like 1969-1970. I actually graduated in 1971.

I was fighting for freedom, blue jeans and all. This was the time of the peace movement and Vietnam and to do wild things. One wild thing was for me to show up at school with blue jeans. That was prohibited.

I would fight for many things considered radical at the time because I was fighting for freedom. I wanted to wear what I wanted to wear. I wanted to do what I wanted to do.

When I was voted class president, the administration pulled

the election and had everybody elect another class president; they re-elected another guy. They made me vice-president. They couldn't have me running everything, but I could hold high spots within the student council. We still finagled things that we wanted. Most of the time I wasn't at school anyway.

I went to Europe (for the summer as a foreign exchange student). Who knows how I got into this program with terrible grades I had. I was in Europe with a bunch of nuns and kids. We went to London, throughout Europe, and into France.

Charles de Gaulle was the President and military leader of France at that time. We met his right-hand man. It was all supposed to be educational. We had these nuns for our chaperones.

I had a blast there.

In Holland, we lived on a ship for a few days. I convinced the nuns that I wanted the other kids to experience culture in Holland at night time and asked if we could we please go out?

I looked fairly old. I had a little goatee on, so they agreed and said, "Oh sure, it would be delightful to show the kids the culture."

They let me be in charge and we had a blast. I took the kids out to a bar and started drinking with everybody in Holland.

Another time we went to concerts where they had big racks of hash. You went up to a guy and said, "Yeah, I want hash." He had a big knife and cut off a big hunk. It was inexpensive, five bucks maybe.

I had a fun time with my fake ID. It got me into all different types of fun things.

Party Entrepreneurs

When my parents would leave on the weekends, we would buy quarter barrels of beer with our fake IDs. We would invite our high school to the party and charge them to go into my parents' house. My parents' house had a basement and two-stories, so it was a pretty big house.

On Friday night, my parents would pull out to go hunting. I said that I had to stay home because I was a part of the church group. I was part of the church group, but I only did it so that I could get out of stuff like going on the weekends with my parents. I didn't hunt, so they figured, "Oh, isn't this nice that Randy is being a good church boy?"

My friends would all be waiting a block away and have one person watching at the end of the block to see when my parents pulled out of the driveway. Once my parents left our house, they drove a few blocks down and then made a left to go onto the highway. That's when we started a patrol with all these kids' cars pulling into our driveway; then the party started. Whenever my parents went somewhere, within five minutes we had the party started. We had barrels of beer, ice, and everything. We would normally charge on Friday night. We'd charge them a buck each to get in. They could have all the beer they wanted to drink.

We made hundreds of dollars. At every party, we paid for all the beer that we wanted and still made money. We had all this excess money and used it to go and have even more fun.

On Saturday night, we sometimes had a formal dinner. We used my parents' formal china, put the extensions in the table, added a white tablecloth, and those who had a date would sit at the table. We had a dozen people at the big table.

We had another table in the breakfast room where we sat about six people. They were all couples, and if you were a UB member who didn't have a date, you would be the waiter.

Johnny, this best friend of mine, was a good cook. He was interested in cooking. We would fix beef tenderloin and all this delicious food, and it would be served to us.

After dinner, we partied with the music going full out. My dad had this big stereo system throughout the house. We would play rock-and-roll, the Beatles, whatever, and just have a blast. That was part of our fun, but at the same time we couldn't get caught.

Clean-up and Fix-it Masters

The main reason why we didn't get caught is that, my brothers, when I was maybe 10 years old, would have parties at the house, too. They would allow me to come, with a couple of my friends, as long as I did all the cleaning up afterwards. So, I took a little beer, had a little fun, and loved being around all these people. They would leave the place a mess.

One time I wasn't there to clean up. I had to go with my parents. When I opened up my bedroom, the bunk beds where my younger brother and I slept were pushed down on their sides. There were rubbers laying in our room, beer cans, it was wrecked. They had forgotten to clean my room.

Anyway, I was the cleaner. I became a master cleaner along with my friends. We learned how to clean. When we had our parties, my mother would come home and say, "You know this house is cleaner than when I left. I wonder if they had some kind of party or something here."

In fact, we were smoking cigarettes in there, so we had to air out the whole house. We were master fixers, too. I shared how we fixed the boat.

At one party, we were drunk and as young teenagers we were wild and had all this energy. My family had bought this beautiful little marble table. I think it was from Italy. It was a beautifully carved wooden base that this marble was sitting on. Someone sat on it and broke it. We were doing all the partying and beer until two or three o'clock in the morning. Then we would start cleaning up because it was Sunday morning. My parents would get back Sunday afternoon.

We had a workbench that we took the table out to. We couldn't fix it the way it was, so we had to saw off about three inches of the wooden base. We put the marble back on the new shorter table. My parents never figured out that the table was shorter.

We had holes in the walls we had to repair. I mean all kinds of things. We spent the rest of the night from 3:00 am to 6:00 am, cleaning up.

During all of it, I was on a high, floating on a cloud, knowing this is how life should be, having this joy, this freedom, this happiness. We had a marvelous time from dinner table parties to making money to being out on the river.

We also had a farm where we would go up and hang out and drop acid. We would sit up on a hillside with all the open air, the trees, the meadow, the wildlife, and the blue sky and trip out. We were in the late 60s, early 70s and this was the hippie time. I was a "hippie" and having a great time.

I went to Wauwatosa East High School. This was a relatively big city. There was Milwaukee, and the nearest suburb was Wauwatosa where I lived. This was an upscale neighborhood that was the first out there. I had a fairly large high school and graduating class. I really never had any prejudice about skin color.

Why? It was 100% white.

The only blacks we did have, were typically exchange students from some country, and I thought they were really good people. I really never got the prejudice at all. I figured people are people, and they are. I wasn't raised with much prejudice. I think one of the reasons is there wasn't too much diversity around there. Nobody was talking negative about any race or color.

Chapter 9

Communicating with Source

There is always an option.

My best solution for the drama of my high school years, for the time I experienced so much contrast, was to enlist in the Army. Again contrast. I'm the hippie guy. I'm the guy who is all about peace, love, and no war.

The UB was astounded. They couldn't believe that, I, of all people, would join the Army. For me, it was my best shot. It was the only solution that I could figure out. This was a way to repay the financial debt for the abortion and a way to go to college. The GI bill would pay for my college.

It would be a way for me to get away from all this contrast and start a new life. I needed to start a new life.

The good news for all of us is that when each of us is at that point of despair, there is always a solution. Recognize that there is a solution, and your Source will guide you to this solution.

Know that when you are in the middle of a situation, you tense up and get scared, you stop breathing. A better action is to relax, breathe deeply, and then ask for what you want.

Ask and you shall receive.

So ask, "What is the solution? How can I get out of this and go to a better place?"

All of us want to get to a better place. There is a better feeling place. And we can all get there by relaxing, breathing deeply, and then asking, "Show me the way. Give me the solution. Give me the answer. I am open to that."

Allow yourself to receive, and you will receive all the solutions. No matter what your situation.

Focus on What You Want

My solution after high school, after totaling a car, being in debt, getting my girlfriend pregnant, not having a good GPA, was the Army. I don't know if there's anybody who could have gotten out of high school in worse shape than I did. Clearly, this led me to the military which gave me this amazing experience, and which paid for my college. I ended up going to the University of Wisconsin, in Medicine no less. The best college in Wisconsin and one of the best in the United States. What a great solution I received!

I never dreamt I could get accepted there. I got accepted and had straight A's in the first semester. How did that happen? Well, that happened because all I did was focus on what I wanted.

For each one of us, focus on whatever you want and you can do it. We all are geniuses. When you are focused that genius comes to the forefront. When you are focused on a particular topic of what you want to be or do, it's possible. As long as you focus on what you do want, you will have it, because there's two sides to every equation.

If you want a college degree, focus and you will have it. I'm not saying that you need a college degree to be successful. A lot of people don't have any degree. We don't need degrees or anything. All we need is that focus.

For most of us, there are two sides to want. One side is focusing on the lack of it or not having it, and the other side is focusing on the want.

A great example is money. People who want money, usually have thoughts filled with the lack of money, they are focused on the fact that they don't have enough money. They go to the mall and they look and they say, "I can't buy this, I can't buy that. I don't have the money."

Whether you are aware of it or not, when you say you can't buy it that is what you are asking for. When lack is asked for then you end up being unable to purchase because you don't have the money.

When you start being on the other side of the wanting there is plenty of money. Consider saying, "This is an abundant world, and I have the power to tap into all the abundance of the Universe. There's plenty of money for me."

When I go shopping, whether I have the actual dollars in my pocket or not is irrelevant. I say things like, "I like that. I'd like to have that. I may get that. I could buy that if I wanted to."

With that attitude, when you see a nice car driving by, like a Bentley, say, "I really like that," instead of saying, "Oh, I wonder how those people got that. They are probably selling drugs to get it."

What you do is you look at it clearly. What do I want? I want that Bentley. I have the power to have that. I love that car. Then go start looking at it. Go test drive it, get pictures of it, go put it on the wall. The more that you can be exposed to the things that you do want, the more you will have what you want.

Take a look at all those challenges I had in high school before I went into the Army. The Army is still paying dividends for me. Most people say, "Oh, the Army doesn't pay much."

Well, it paid me enough. It supplied the bedding, a roof over my head, and food. With the little money I had, within a year and a half, I paid off all my financial debt.

It's paying dividends to me still to this day, and I'm 62 years old. I have the Veterans' Administration; the VA pays for all my medical bills. Not one penny have I paid for medical.

It's all because of the situation I was in, and what I chose to be the solution. My solution out of high school not only brought me to the place that I am now, but it also continues to pay other dividends, too. It gave me discipline and all of those wonderful experiences.

Even when it appears like the solution isn't an ideal solution, you can create it to be the ideal solution. Speak as though it is the ideal situation. It will take you to the next step; not always that immediate solution, but it will take you to the solution for all of your dreams to come true.

I know this. I've been blessed to know through the experiences that I have had. God (Source) doesn't talk to us in English, doesn't talk to us in Spanish or any language.

Source is energy.

It is this energy, together with our thoughts, that we can use to mold the energy of the Universe. The energy that creates the world is ours to create with. We have the ability and the right to mold it into whatever we want.

When we ask in English (in words), what that asking does is send out a signal to our Source. The Source immediately answers that signal. We need to stay focused on that signal.

In other words, we need to stay focused on that thought of what we want during the day. Our prayers are said when we are on our hands and knees and our hands are folded. It is quiet. It is typically clear in our mind what we are focused on in prayer. The physical position of our body helps to focus our thoughts. However, as we ask and pray during the day, our thoughts can go in random zigzags. Asking is impacted by the world we are inhabiting and the people around us.

Yellow + Red = Orange

Think of it this way in colors.

If I ask for more money, let's call that the color yellow. Then during the day, when I think about my need for more money, I think of it this way:

Why don't I have money to pay my bills?
Why don't I have enough money to pick up that nice car?
Why do my expenses go up and my income stays the same?

Let's call that asking red.

First, I asked for yellow. Now, I'm asking for red. When you put yellow and red together, you get orange.

Anyone who has ever asked for anything, usually ends up saying to themselves, "I asked for yellow, but I got orange. Aren't you listening? I didn't ask for orange."

But the fact is, you did ask for orange because you were asking for the yellow on wanting money and then the red on not wanting money. The signal that responds is orange.

It is us sending out mixed signals, not Source who isn't listening.

When I send out the signal, Source answers me. Source answers me with energy and that energy goes into my mind, and it translates it into a thought.

The choices I made when I was 17 years old were the result of me asking, "What in the hell should I do? Do I go to this little rich boy's school?" The answer I heard was, "No."

You know, the reason I resisted going to the little rich boy's school is that I didn't feel good about it. See, when we don't feel good, we lose our connection.

We don't need an ancient book such as the Bible to know what God's talking about or telling us. This is a personal experience we all have with God, and it's through our emotions that God speaks to us.

When we're not thinking the same way that God's thinking about a topic, we feel bad. When we are alignment with God's thinking for us, we feel good. When I was thinking about a topic of going to the rich boy's college, that didn't make me feel good, so that means that was not my path.

What was my path? I could have taken the option of being in Vegas and doing what Ann Otis offered to give me. I would have been a card dealer or a blackjack dealer, in one of the casinos, but that didn't sound right to me either. It didn't feel good.

I didn't feel good being unsure whether Jennifer was in love with me. I believed that we wouldn't be together for long before she would be like her mother and we would end up being divorced.

What did make me feel good was joining the Army.

I really liked this solution. It was the Source that gave me the idea to go into the military. Believe me, none of my friends were thinking about me going into the military. I wasn't thinking of going into the military. I was a hippie against war and stood for peace and love. I didn't want any part of the military.

But when the idea came, I loved the idea. It got me away from Wisconsin. I had a job, and I wanted to experience war; not to die in it, but to experience that contrast.

At the time, I didn't realize it, but what I was looking for was the experience and to explore.

The Source guided me, telling me, "You are going to be here longer. You are not going to Vietnam and die like so many war heroes did."

Bless them. I'm so grateful for them. I know people who died because they served in the military. Some neighbors of mine passed away. May they always be remembered.

There is freedom in knowing there really is no death here. We think that they're not here, but they are here.

For me to realize that in my asking, all of a sudden, I got this idea of the military. That is huge. Think about it. I have orders for Vietnam, and in the same week that I am supposed to be leaving for Vietnam, my orders get changed, and I have this remarkable experience in Korea.

It was all divinely orchestrated. Simply be in a receptive mode to receive and be led on your Lighted path.

Deliberate Choices

It is important for us to care most about how we feel. It is important that we are deliberate. Every day I wake up and say, "My dominant intent is to feel good, and I seek and find things today that help make me feel good."

Do this, and you will be on your lighted path and you will thrive. As you thrive, the whole world will thrive along with you.

I knew, even at age 17, that going into the military would definitely give me discipline. I had heard about that, and I was ready for it. Even though I didn't want my dad to ever tell me another fucking thing to do, I knew needed somebody to tell me.

I had drill sergeants in basic training. They told me what to do, and I did it. I did it with excellence, and I was trained for that. As far as good grades were concerned, I wasn't there yet, but when I got out of the military, then my focus was on education and I wanted to get good grades.

Like I said, in my first semester I got straight A's in college. Going from 1.8 to straight A's was only a matter of focus.

We each have this ability to get good grades. Feel yourself moving from whatever feels good to be directed there, then, that direction will take you to the next step.

At the time, did I want a new experience? Yes. I wanted discipline. For me to choose discipline was definitely something new. Yet somehow I knew I needed discipline. And I also knew this would be a financially freeing path, too.

The How is God's Business

It's still an option for anybody to have a job and get that discipline, to see the world, and then from there who knows where it will take you. One of the things that trips us up is some of us get too caught up in 'the how', asking "How am I going to do that?"

'The how' isn't your business. If you have the desire, you will be led to what you want. If you try to make it happen, you can never figure it out. I would have never figured out to choose the military after high school. I figured out what I wanted and Source provided the solution.

All of these highs and lows and God was there the whole time. I could feel God's presence in the highs. I could feel God's presence in the lows.

No way would I have predicted that enlisting in the Army would have taken me to the University of Wisconsin and straight A's.

How could I have known that my choice of schools would take me to Procter and Gamble (P&G), because they only interview in certain schools?

How would I have known that they always choose the Midwest and the University of Wisconsin where people have heart? That was P&G's philosophy.

Before the military, I never would have believed that I could have been hired by Procter and Gamble, let alone tell them, "I want to go to Florida," and they would move me to Florida (so I could get out of the winter).

I never could have figured out that would be my path. What a magnificent, amazing, brilliant and wonderful path to be on!

Each of us has experienced our own amazing, brilliant, wonderful path, but most of us are still thinking about the bad stuff that has happened to us, and we make that our focus. I turned my painful childhood into my new story, about how grateful I am. My new story includes high school and the tragedy of the car accident, and the fun and wonderful times, too.

> *Oh, my God, I am so appreciative of all the things that happened to me at the end of high school. Because, it took me getting out of high school at a low to reach the amazing, brilliant, and wonderful place that I call heaven right here on earth.*
>
> *The happy life that I'm living is a result of my ability to follow my good feelings and know that my bad feelings are what I don't want. My good feelings, which come from the Source in me, are what I follow to have my dreams come true. Each of us can find happiness in all we seek. We have the freedom to choose which feelings we are going to focus on.*

Know that we are here for more freedom and growth. Think of all the growth you have had. Think of all the freedom that you desire and how you can have that. Focus on what you want.

Each of us is looking for growth and freedom to choose whatever we want to do. Be disciplined. If you want to choose to have fun, you can have it all. You know you can have fun.

> *I have fun, but at the same time I'm disciplined in a loving and easy way. I no longer have a little military drill sergeant in my head saying, "You've got to do this." I go where it feels good.*

> *That's my discipline now. It's a whole new level of discipline that I go to now to follow those good feelings. That keeps me on the path of great opportunities for myself. The prize in doing that is freedom.*

You have the ability to choose what you want and to get it. You can ask for it and you can get it. It is so powerful to recognize that you can have it. Now, will it happen the moment you think about it? No, but be happy about that, too!

Everything Doesn't Manifest Right Away

Think of the thoughts you've had that could have manifested right away in your life. The point is, as we get that energy going and focus on what we do want, it clears that open, lighted path for us to easily and in a fun way, start skipping down the path of joy and abundance.

Besides the prize of freedom, there is also a prize for the joy you will experience! I look at all of those experiences in high school, especially towards the end, that gave me more joy. I experienced more growth, more freedom, and more joy.

I am not unique!

You have the power to have all of this, and all of your dreams to come true, as well!

God does not discriminate!

There was no way I could have figured out beforehand that I would go into the military with low pay and within a year and a half pay off all of my debt.

I sat at the end of high school wondering, "How do I get food on the table? How do I get a roof over my head?" Wondering how to pay off my debt was barely a thought.

The Source had all the solutions, and before I knew it, I was out of debt. That's why, when we are being led, and we feel good, if we start having thoughts and second guessing, that's going to take away and get us off the path.

If you have faith and trust, and know that everything is going to play out to your benefit, then it will come even faster to you.

The Bible says, "Your cup runneth over."

What does that mean? It means that whatever you ask for, you get even more.

So, I asked. I wanted my freedom. I got my freedom. I wanted financially to pay off debt, I got that. I received that and so much more! I had the amazing Mafia experience, and was given the highest non-combat award by the United States Army, the Army Commendation Medal.

I traveled the world and saw different things. It paid for my college.

I had no idea that Congress would sign a bill saying that Vietnam Veterans will have all their health care paid. That happened within the last 10 years or so.

I am many years out of the Army and the benefits continue to flow into my life. There's no way I could have figured that out at age 17. Think about how much money that gives me, to have my medical paid for life.

That's what happens when you stay on track, and you say you feel good, and you believe that you are going to be led. You're given those thoughts like magnets. We will attract whatever we are thinking about.

Attract Harmonious People to You

You will attract people to you who will help you to bring you to your desires. Nobody gets used. It's all harmonious and you can bring that to you!

Therefore, we are all in the middle of our own Universe and we attract from the whole Universe. We attract the people, the circumstances, the events and situations.

What are you going to do?

It's time for you to start thinking about what you want. Discipline yourself to only think about what you want, and then have the faith and the belief that God's going to deliver it to you, plus more! That's how amazing each one of us is!

What brilliant, magnificent creators we are. As you become a deliberate creator, you can have all of your dreams come true. You can have all harmonious people, all the money, the perfect lover, the best career.... It's all right there!

Everything that you want as long as you're thinking about it, is coming to you. We are all magnets. It's as though you're a semiconductor, and you have that magic wand in your hand. That magic wand is your thoughts, and it can contour and mold the energy that creates the world into your experience and the people and things you want; everything you want to do, be, and have.

You have this wand. All you have to do is put it in your hand, lift the wand up, and a whole symphony of nonphysical is sitting there waiting for your direction. They will go and get you whatever you want, and there is no judgment.

That's why, when you're thinking you're poor that you get more poor, because they are going to give you whatever you want.

Who are they? They are that Source energy, God, your angels, your guides. That's all those who have walked before you. All of your answers. They are all interested in what you are doing right now and what you are thinking.

They want nothing more than to guide you to all of your desires because they know that joy is the prize for everyone. It's for us to focus on what brings in the joy.

Ask yourself, what do I desire?

Then focus on that side of the coin, and just that side of the coin on any and every subject.

Then everything that you want will come to you.

Chapter 10

Seeing and Feeling the Love All Around Me

I was born into a family with a loving father. He did the best job that he could to love me, help me, and in his mind to ensure that I would have a long, happy, and prosperous life which I have had!

My mother loved me, too. She loved me dearly. I would have wonderful conversations with my mother sitting out on the grass or in the kitchen. She gave me more love when we were alone than probably any other person. I had better discussions with her than I ever had with any other person.

My grandparents were loving, in particular my grandmother who was especially nice. She would take me on bus rides. She would buy me teddy bears.

My other grandparents were wonderful, as well. I would go into their bedroom in the afternoon and watch TV and fall asleep there without anyone waking me up. They loved that. In fact, Grandma would put a little blanket over me, and give me a little kiss on my forehead. She thought I was sleeping, but I could feel her gentle touch and her kindness as she wrapped her love around me. I loved them so much. I had a fun and wonderful upbringing and I had wonderful friends.

Discovering Power Within Love

On the playground growing up, we played a variation of tag that started with everybody on one side of the playground. Only one person was alone in the middle of the playground. All the other kids lined up on the one side and ran from that side to the other not wanting to get tagged by the person in the middle. When the person in the middle tagged someone, he or she would be in the middle, too. Then both of them would tag someone who was running across the field.

Eventually, it would be that there was only one person left who didn't get tagged. On one particular day, I was the only person left who wasn't tagged.

All the other kids lined up in front of me trying to tag me before I could get to the other side. Wouldn't you know it, I dodged and ditched and went every which way until I finally reached the other side without being tagged! Oh my God, I felt great. It was a glorious time to me.

I had experiences, too, where I was more empowered than ever. I discovered my own power within me, and I had this amazing childhood where my brothers loved to play together and we were doing everything they wanted to do, go out, play, have fun, and be free.

I appreciate those fun, play-filled memories about my dear loving brothers. I appreciate my mother and my father, too. After all, I know that we chose our parents before we arrived here. I'm happy I made the right decision. I picked the most loving parents. I truly appreciate the parents and the brothers who helped me get to this place where I am right now where I express more freedom than I ever would have without them.

I have emotions and feelings of new heights, a new reality that I live in that I would not have had if it weren't for those wonderful loving people in my life. Without those wonderful experiences in my life, I wouldn't have known that I am this magnificent, beautiful, loving creator with a purpose to expand all that is and that I'm doing a wonderful job at that expansion.

Everything is perfect, and it's going to continue to expand. When I transition from my physical being to my non-physical being, I will expand into that beautiful consciousness even more. If I decide to come back, I will. There is no big deal. I don't need to be protected by anything. I create the experiences that I want in my life. I've decided to create this abundant life of mine. This life with more feelings of abundance, of freedom, of the prize of it all, of joy. I experience all of this because I changed my story.

Look for the Good

In the story I live today, I look for the good because there is good and there is love in everything. I now focus on the things that are good and loving. When I look at my past, I only pay attention to the things that I want, and I don't talk about the things that I don't want.

I don't go to a pity party anymore. If you have pity parties, stop inviting everybody. Stop the pity party altogether and decide to go have fun. Enjoy this beautiful life that is waiting for you. Experience all of this abundance, freedom, and joy that is awaiting you right now.

Chapter 11

My Mother

When Father was in the house, my mother would hide and not say anything. Even she was scared of him; terrified actually. I was born before the Peace Movement and Women's Lib. Women were supposed to get married, have children, stay home, manage the house, be the mom, and shut up. My father's attitude, like many men's attitudes of that day was, "You don't have anything to say. You do whatever I say."

It was an entirely different world then and a different culture. When Mom and I were together, we had these amazing talks and wonderful times. We might be right in the middle of a conversation when my dad would come in, and immediately she was out of there.

I always knew I was in trouble when he told her, "Get out of here, Shirleen. I'm going to handle this." Most of the time, I never knew what I did wrong. When he left me out on the road, I never knew why. I really didn't understand any of it.

Liberation

My mother couldn't wait for my youngest brother to graduate from high school because she was going to get out. By this time, women's liberation started to have an influence on women. Back then, you didn't get a divorce even if it was really bad, because "you could handle it." But my mom saw other couples divorce and she herself couldn't wait to get a divorce. Mother left my dad the same day my youngest brother left the house.

Who did my dad call?

Me. My father cried to me. I went to him and helped him through that whole divorce. It goes to show that when you respect yourself, others will respect you. When you allow other people to disrespect you, then you'll be disrespected. It's a vicious cycle.

My dad was shocked that she would leave, but why would he be? When I was a teenager, they were in separate bedrooms. Once a month, my dad would go in and have sex with her. When I say, "have sex," he had a climax, but she didn't. She couldn't wait for him to get out of the room. That was their love life.

There were other things going on, too, like my father having an affair with his secretary.

His secretary was my mom's best friend.

Mom and her friend would have martinis at 4 o'clock every day and I'm sure both of them knew what was going on, but neither was talking about it. Mom suffered continual disregard and disrespect from my father.

I was happy for my mother; happy that she freed herself. Like me, in the process she became the 'light' and gained respect from my father, too. I believe my standing up to my father had significant influence on my mother as well. I gave her the strength to do this.

When she left, she really had no place to go other than to live in the attic of her parents' house. She had dropped out of college and supported my dad when he was going to school. She never got a degree and she didn't have any formal job, other than she was a beautiful model when she was young. When she left my dad, she was older and modeling wasn't an option.

Feeling Good, Feeling Bad, and Choosing Your Path

My mother was a beautiful model. She modeled for Seven Group in different high-end shows. She easily was the most beautiful, desirable girl in town. My father was a handsome soldier, a big bomber who eventually returned home as a decorated World War II hero released from prison camp. Theirs was a match made in Heaven. Or, maybe not.

The night before she was to marry my dad, my mother confided to her girlfriend that she wasn't sure she should be getting married. She was concerned about having known my dad for only six months. She said, "I don't know if I'm going to love this guy. What am I doing here? Oh, he is a big military hero, and I'm this pretty model, but what if this isn't right?"

She didn't stick with her true feelings, and got married, even though she questioned whether it was the right decision. She really wasn't in love with him; he swept her off her feet. That he did do, but she wasn't in love with him. He was a great talker, a great communicator, a great persuader. He convinced her that getting married was what she wanted when really it was what he wanted. From early on, being married to my dad wasn't what she wanted.

> *Whenever I hear that small voice of question whispering, "I don't know if this is right," I get out of it. Or at the least, I pause, listen, and question the situation and solution.*

When you are in a situation and you feel despair or you feel you can't get out of the situation, I assure you there is another, better solution for you. Everything will be better if you take the steps necessary to get out of that situation.

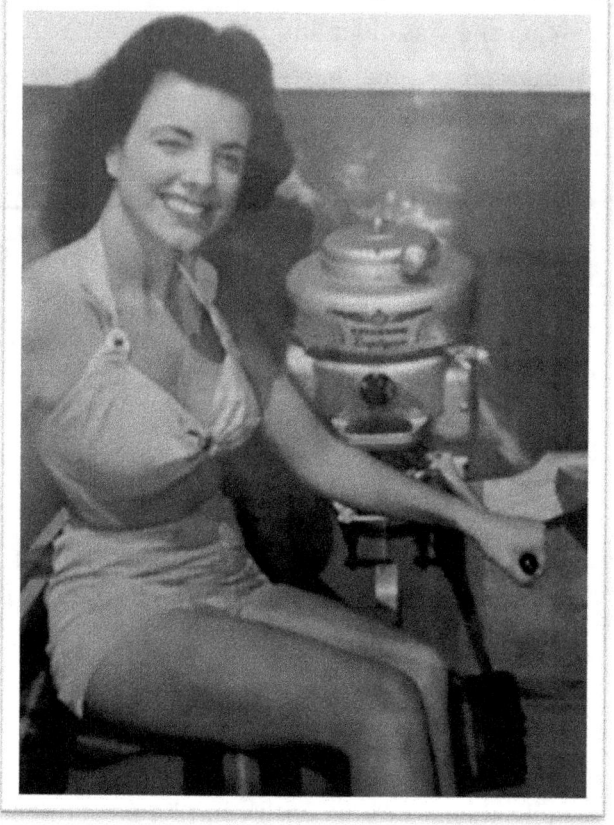

It doesn't matter if it's a divorce or a job you hate or if it's abuse from your family, whatever it is, get out of it. You'll get the money you need, there will be plenty. We live in a world of plenty. Recognize that there's plenty of everything; plenty of love, plenty of money, plenty of resources. As you recognize this is a world of plenty, then it makes perfect sense that you can call forth what you want.

You have the power to call forth. It won't necessarily be the next hour or the next day, but when you make the decision about what you do want and then listen to that inner voice within you, you will be guided directly to the solution.

The voice isn't a voice in English or Spanish, it is a feeling. You will find that there are only two feelings: there's good feeling and bad feeling. It's easy to discern which feelings you want to listen to and move towards.

The good feeling, tells you that you're on the path to what you want. You're on your lighted path. You're on the path toward what your Source wants. Your Source wants what you want. What you ask for, your Source is going to deliver.

When you feel bad at any time and in any situation, be sensitive to your feelings. When you feel bad, take a moment and recognize that you are not on your best path. Then ask, "How can I get on my lighted path? How can I get to the things that I want because this is what I don't want?" Look at what you don't want and clearly recognize that this is not what you want. Then ask, "What do I want?"

When you are clear about what you do want and you ask for what you want, then the answers will be given. You send a vibration out to your Source and then the answers come back from your Source. You are answered immediately. Your Source is sending vibrations that turn into thoughts that guide you to what is next. You will then start attracting the people, the circumstances, and events that get you what you want.

Seeking Freedom

I don't think my father was physically abusive to my mother, but he was incredibly emotionally abusive and degrading; that is far worse than physical abuse ever would be. Our emotions come from our inner world, and it's our feelings that are our communication connection with Source. Emotional abuse totally messes with our spirit, our soul and our ability to create what we want.

Too often, people will say, "Oh well, she wasn't physically abused." Emotional abuse leaves more scars than physical abuse ever will. Bones heal, hearts don't.

Mom was emotionally abused and beaten down to the point that she accepted being treated as a "thing." She was told where to go, what to do, and when to spread her legs. That's how she was treated.

Ultimately, each of us is seeking freedom.

That's why you can never put anyone in chains, or worse yet, isolation. You can physically put them in chains, you can emotionally put them chains, but ultimately, freedom will rise to the top. It may not be this year, it may not be in this generation, but it will in time. It's all because each one of us desires more freedom. Yes, my mother was emotionally abused down to a thing. And that is why she left as soon as she felt she could.

We Were Not Allowed to Share Feelings

My father was also abusive to his mother. Grandmother was a dear, sweet woman to me, and I loved her. She took me for my first bus ride, and I was astounded by the sights. We went downtown around the big buildings. (This was in Milwaukee, Wisconsin in the 60s so you know they weren't too big.) I spent an amazing day with Grandmother. She took me shopping and bought me an adorable little teddy bear. I loved this little teddy bear. I hugged it all the way home.

I had one of the best days of my young life. I came home, walked into the door with my little teddy bear, and my dad said to her, "What the hell? What the hell do you think you're doing buying stuff for this damn kid?"

And, before I knew it, he ripped the teddy bear from my grip, and threw it in the garbage. I never saw that teddy bear again.

Anything and everything triggered the constant anger in my father and subsequent abuse. Growing up, we didn't talk about any of this, and certainly never our feelings. He would often say, "Hey, no feelings!"

We were not allowed to have feelings. He really didn't share anything about himself, but I do know he was an only child.

I don't think he was given too much love by his father. That's probably where he picked up his dysfunctional behavior about not showing love.

I imagine that his father abused his mother and that is the pattern he grew up with. He abused his mother, my mom, and his four children. It wasn't abuse in his mind—he thought he was right. Most of the time, he wasn't even thinking. To him, it was, "What the hell? It was only a teddy bear. Who cares?"

He refused to allow use to have anything to do with pleasing or pleasant experiences. We weren't going to have any of "that" in our life.

CHAPTER 12

Shifting Momentum to Change Your Life

We have the power to change any current momentum that isn't playing out on our behalf. Let's say we have a relationship where the person doesn't trust us, isn't kind to us, or is controlling us. Any situation that we're in, we have the power to stop the momentum and shift direction.

Do you find yourself feeding the momentum? Do you hear yourself making statements like these?

They don't trust me.
They don't believe me.
They are mean to me.

If so, then shift direction. You can say positive things like:

I see they are more endearing with me.
They believe me.
They say kind things to me.

You have the power to change people. We've been told, "You can't change other people." That completely is not the case.

I help people change their relationships with others all the time, and I've done that with myself. The way it's done is to start looking at yourself. Think about yourself in the way you want to see you, not the way that you are now perhaps, not the way that you've been, but how you want to see yourself, how you want to be.

Perhaps you think that there is so much negative momentum that you can't stop it, you can't change it. When you are in the midst of a situation's momentum, recognize that you can change the momentum by changing the way that you look at the situation, the people, and yourself. You might feel that the momentum is like a car going fast down the hill and you can't get in front of it. Maybe it feels like you're about to be run over. Whatever the case is, what you do is stop paying attention to it completely.

Yes. Stop paying attention to it. To do that, shift your attention to something that you do want. For example, focus your attention on other relationships.

As you begin to create the power of positive, encouraging, uplifting, loving, harmonious relationships, what will happen is the bad relationship will start turning around as well. You are now creating momentum leading toward what you want. You will attract more of the things that you want, and that momentum snowball of receiving what you want will get bigger and bigger.

That principle is called the Law of Attraction.

Like attracts like, and you will start to create that momentum for what you want. You create where you want the momentum to go.

Be Clear About What You Want and Pay Attention

I created exactly where I wanted the momentum to go in my life: lots of money, a $1,000,000 home, spending money on trips and lots of material things. The more I spent, the more I needed. The higher my positions, the higher the stress.

Eventually the momentum was too much, and I had to get out. I wasn't paying attention as I should have been. I knew things were off-kilter a bit; however, I was too caught up in the momentum to realize just how far off-kilter things were.

That's how I created a truck going 60 miles an hour to hit me while I was completely stopped by a school bus.

The impact broke my neck and left me in a coma.

Chapter 13

Healing Myself from a Broken Neck

Healing myself from the excruciating pain of a broken neck really was one step at a time, one moment at a time. I didn't say, "Hey, I want to be totally out of pain, and I expect it right now." Instead, I asked myself to think about how it feels to NOT be in pain. I started thinking about how it would feel to have clarity (instead of being confused because of all the drugs they were pumping into my blood system through the IV). I asked myself to feel clear, to have crisp clarity, and to be of clear mind.

Then I started to imagine how it felt to have freedom. I *imagined* freedom until I could *experience* the feeling of freedom and how good it felt for me. I felt that freedom in my spirit. I felt that clarity. I felt that goodness.

It took a lot of discipline to focus on the good. It always does. I disciplined my thoughts.

I didn't allow myself to think about how bad my health was, because that would create this momentum of even worse health.

I was grabbing for the feeling of being healthy and feeling well to have clarity of mind and to have freedom. Gradually, I began to grasp the feelings I wanted, good feelings of health, clarity, and the vitality of freedom.

As I felt those feelings, the day finally came when there was one moment where I felt energized. I felt clear. I felt that freedom. I hung onto that one moment. I disregarded the day's other 23 hours and 59 minutes of pain and confusion. Though it was one fleeting moment, I knew I could create it again. I knew I could experience more instances of that feeling.

When I first started this journey to health, I didn't have any moments of feeling good. I could only imagine it. I remember asking God to expand my imagination so that I could see the way I wanted my life to be, the way I wanted me to be, and the way that I wanted to feel good. I wanted to feel this health, this clarity, this freedom.

When my reality did not include even one second during the day of what I wanted to feel, I used my imagination to create how it would feel to have it. Day after day, I focused on how it felt to be free and healthy, to have vitality and clarity.

One step, one day at a time, I built momentum from imagining and visually feeling well to physically feeling well and being where I wanted to be. I realized that I had to build one step at a time. It was one moment at a time and I had to only focus on how good that moment of health felt, and to disregard what I didn't want.

Soon it became two minutes that I could enjoy during the day. Then, there were three minutes a day, and then there were more. Soon there was an hour of being healthy, of having clarity, of feeling so good. The momentum began to build and carry me in the direction I wanted to go.

I could imagine myself on a large wave in Hawaii, surfing a wave and streaming down with momentum of good health, clarity, and freedom. I felt the harmonious people and all the wonderful things that I wanted in my life. I rode the momentum down that beautiful wave and slid in front of that big beautiful blue wave with those white caps. I was going down easy. Before I knew it, I was feeling the joy 24 hours a day.

Stop Fighting for Lack and Limitation

For 10 years after the car accident, I suffered from horrendous headaches. The C1 and C2 vertebrae in my spinal cord were broken in the accident. Literally the stem of my brain was hitting C1 and C2 at the top of my neck. That was creating excruciating headaches.

Doctors were telling me that in order for the stem of my brain not to hit C1 and C2, they would need to put a rod down my neck. "Sure," they said, "you'll never move your neck left or right again, but so what?"

I resisted their recommendations. What the doctors offered was all the stuff that I didn't want! It took me 10 full years after the accident before I woke up one day and realized that I didn't have a throbbing migraine or tremendous pain the whole day.

In all of those 10 years, every day I focused my attention towards feeling good. I disregarded what I didn't want. Sometimes, I would point to it (I didn't want to give it too much emotional attention), and I would say, "Headache, migraine, pain beyond belief, you are not real. You are what I don't want. I appreciate you and am grateful because you are birthing what I do want, you are birthing this pure health, this feeling of being on top of the world, this feeling of living in the clouds."

I now have my head in the clouds and my feet rooted deeply in the ground. It's all because of the visualization I've been doing for the last 10 years or more.

You may say, "I don't want to wait 10 years to be rid of my migraines or pain."

You don't have to wait 10 years. You can create, be, do and have anything you want. It's all a matter of how much are you going to allow? How much are you going to receive? Because there is only wellbeing that flows through us. When that concept, that understanding, that knowing is understood, there's only good that flows to us. The only thing that cuts our good and our wellbeing off is our own thoughts and feelings.

If you raise your hands above your head and you spread them out wide and allow that wellbeing, there will be pure health that flows through you. You can be healthy at the snap of the fingers. But, for most of us, because we have been brought up to believe it isn't possible, and because we honor the god with the small 'g' (the god of other people's opinions), we don't manifest what we want as quickly as we could.

How many doctors think they are some kind of God?

They are not God. They don't do any of the healing. When they do an operation, they do it, and they sew you up. Who's doing the healing in that? It's no doctor. It is this wellbeing that flows to us. With your hands spread wide and your arms wide open, you open the flow of your Source.

If you start to focus on resistant thoughts and start putting your arms and your hands closer and closer together that will cut off this wellbeing from flowing to you.

Stop fighting for your lack and limitation.

Stop arguing for, "I really do have a headache, and I do have this pain." The more you say that, the greater the momentum of your pain is, and the less likely you're going to be released of that and experience good health. We need to awaken and say to ourselves, "I'm going to focus on what I want. I want good health to start flowing to me and through me."

It will be because there's only wellbeing flowing to us. There is no evil out there. The only evil is when we start cutting off our own thoughts of wellbeing. Then, as we look through our physical eyes, we see the world as being bad and painful. We have blocked out the wellbeing, and it becomes clouded and it looks like it's not a good world. It looks like there is pain in this world.

The fact is, all of us have the power to create and allow this wellbeing to flow to us. So to the person who recently had a headache or had some type of physical ailment, I share with you that all things are possible, and that it is possible for you right now to heal yourself.

You have the power. Christ said you have the power. You and I have the power to move mountains. Most of us don't believe that. Most of us believe it's got to be Christ. But Christ told us and showed us, we have that.

We Have the Power

The tenets of all major religions come down to this: there is this magnificent power, and it's in each one of us.

We have the power to create, be, do, and have anything and everything we want including good health, overcoming any situation, and changing any circumstance we have.

How? How do we tap into this power?

You do it one step at a time, thinking good thoughts, imagining the feeling.

Imagine the feeling of good health, imagine the feeling of a good deep, meaningful, loving relationship.

As you start imagining that, it will start.

You are a magnet; each of us is a magnet.

We start attracting to us more and more good feeling thoughts that start creating circumstances, events, and situations that are in alignment with those thoughts.

You can attract things to you that were once beyond your imagination, things that you never could have conceived of before.

This Source energy that most people call God, has the ability and has put it inside of us. It's the power we have with our thoughts, and that same power that creates worlds; we have that power to create the life that we want, the good health, the circumstances, relationships, all the money, all the abundance, and then the prize of it all is joy.

We were meant to come here and have our dreams come true and to experience more freedom and more joy.

It is now up to us.

It's our responsibility to no longer get into that pity party and no longer fight for that lack and limitation. Instead think about who you want to be, and what kinds of experiences you want to have.

It's Between God and You

You ask for it and God will do all the work. God will do the how and bring you these amazing experiences.

This is exactly what took me from the street, being homeless, no money, no roof over my head, no wife.

After the accident, I lost everything in my life; all the riches and my big million-dollar business. Everything was gone, and I took it one breath at a time.

In that one moment, when I created the pain-free moment, that led to the path of my happiness.

My momentum before the accident was not in the direction I wanted. I felt more freedom after I lost everything.

I felt better sleeping in a car than I did sleeping in a million-dollar home with the expensive cars in the garage.

You bet.

Money can bring happiness. All things can. But, when you're not happy, when you have this pressure to produce, and you're not in a happy state, it doesn't matter what you have, you are not going to be happy.

Each of us has the ability to create a state of happiness right now.

You have the ability to feel good in this moment no matter what's going on. If you can hang onto that moment of feeling good, it will take you to everything that you want.

CHAPTER 14

You Can Create a New Story

The contrast that we have in our lives doesn't have to be as severe as the contrast I have experienced in my lifetime. You may be someone who has gone through challenging times in your life. All of us have felt this place of despair and being disempowered at some time in our life; the lowest of all low. We've been there. The lowest vibration (feeling) we can experience is being disempowered, the highest vibration (feeling) is the opposite, empowered.

First of all, embrace those circumstances. Embrace the contrast that shows you the things you don't want that are here to help you birth ideas and provide clarity for what you do want. They are all blessings. Everything that happens in our lives, no matter whether we called it *wanted* or *unwanted*, *good* or *bad*, is here to help us to expand.

That's why each one of us plays a vital role in this world. Each of us is here to expand all that we have experienced into deeper feelings and more thoughts; into feelings that have never been before, yet each one of us have had since birth.

We are born happy. Most of us (if not all of us) have found ourselves unhappy at one time or another. I wanted to commit suicide, not once, but twice. I couldn't handle my life anymore because I was so separated from my Source. I wasn't thinking about my life the way my Source was. That's why I say we have only two feelings. There are good feelings and there are bad feelings.

When I was living these stories, I had those bad feelings because I did not see the experience through the eyes of God. I was looking at my life through the eyes of my smaller self and applying my own interpretation.

For many of us, our story is one of despair and disempowerment. You don't have to stay stuck in that story you created while you were living it.

An Exercise: Change Your Story

I want to share with you an amazing, easy way to change your story. This is a beautiful exercise and a way to transform yourself to start telling a new story about how great your life is.

Directions: Look for one experience every five years of your life that was really, really good. Look for a moment that made your heart sing. Write it down. It can be any story you want. Focus on the abundance, joy and freedom you felt at that time.

With your new story you can birth an event that happened in your life and you can also birth, realize, and understand how this experience births new feelings of abundance, freedom, and of joy.

You've already heard many of the stories of my life, and how bad it was. I didn't feel good when it was happening. I will show you how I can create a new story, appreciating the contrast and seeing the good that was there. Here is my story as an example. I include the feelings of abundance, freedom, and joy in the telling of my story, because these are the three top reasons why we're really here.

My New Story

Age Birth to Five

My grandmother and I were on the bus together. I was so amazed by the big world and the tall buildings in downtown Milwaukee. To me, these were huge skyscrapers. Being there I could feel the joy and excitement and adventure.

My grandmother showed me unconditional love that gave me joy. I also felt free to be myself without fear of repercussion. I felt feelings of freedom, of unconditional love, and my heart was filled with joy when I was with my grandma. She was kind and gentle and loved me so much she bought me a teddy bear to hold and snuggle with. I felt abundance and peace.

> *If you recall that story had a tragic ending with the teddy bear, but don't pay attention to that. Turn the other cheek. When Christ said, "Turn the other cheek," He didn't mean for you to turn the other cheek to get slapped, what He meant was, turn the other cheek so you can change your line of vision and see things differently. Focus on what you want vs. focus on what you don't want.*

Age Five to 10

I felt free being the last kid playing on the playground who wasn't tagged. This was a game all the kids were playing before school started. When everyone was standing in the middle of the field waiting to tag me, I ran straight through without being tagged. I felt euphoric and had an immense feeling of freedom.

I felt free being the last kid standing up by the wall, looking at all the people. I was the only one there.

I said I'm going to make it through all these people (50 to 55 of them), and I did it! I was determined I was going to get through. I was going to dodge and go everywhere or take them out. I was going to get to the other side. I did it!

This experience helped me realize I could start creating things in my life. I didn't realize to the extent that I could create them then, but I realized that, "Wow! When I put my mental focus on something, it comes true!"

Age 10 to 15

Experiencing my first climax in the shower was the best feeling I can remember! I was like, "Oh, this feels so good. This is so wonderful." I decided I want more of this and went on making love to my girlfriend and enjoying how great it was.

Once, we were making love, and I was smoking a cigarette. We were lying on the carpet in the basement. Her mom came down and peeped over the stairs. We could see her. She saw our heads, and so we smiled. I was on top of my girlfriend, and her mom went back upstairs. Who knows what she was thinking. But yeah, that was a fun time.

Age 15 to 20

My new story is about when I was 16. I was a foreign exchange student. I went to Europe and saw more of the world with about 30 really bright kids. Isn't it wonderful that my father was the one who gave me this amazing opportunity to be a foreign exchange student in the summer? I got to go see England and France, and to talk with the Assistant to the French President, Charles de Gaulle.

We met amazing people and had fun times. Because I looked a little older than my age, I convinced the nun who was one of the chaperons to let me take the group out at night in Holland and Amsterdam. I told her that I thought it would be valuable for the students to see the nightlife and understand the culture, maybe meet people. I told her that I understood at her age, she probably did not want to go out at night. So I told her that I would be responsible.

The nun said, "Oh this is a wonderful idea." She was so excited and even said to me, "You would really do that for me?"

I said, "Oh yes, I would."

I took all the kids with me. We went to the first bar and started having beers with the locals. They were all having fun and were appreciative of us young Americans being there. We had a blast and came back fairly drunk around one o'clock in the morning. We snuck in, went to bed, and never got caught. It was a fun time.

> *In this part of my life, I could have told all kinds of contradictory stories. For this exercise in Changing Your Story, you want to stay out of the bad stuff. You'll recall there are many things at 15 to 20 that happened to me, both good and bad. What I don't want to focus on here are things like the car accident and the pregnancy.*

Age 20 to 25

After having a 1.8 GPA in high school, I got straight A's in my first year of college. I made up my mind and focused on what I wanted. We all are geniuses. All we need to do is focus on a subject we want and continue to think about the abundance of that. This was a time when I felt empowered and great about myself.

Age 25 to 30

All kinds of experiences come to mind, but if I were to look at the top one right now, it would be seeing the birth of my first child, Chase. It was almost like a Saturday Night Live skit. This one makes me laugh.

My wife, Mary, was in labor for 23 hours. At this time, fathers weren't allowed in the delivery room, only the doctor and the nurse. Finally, she dilated enough, and the doctor said it was time.

They pushed her down to the delivery room, and I sat in a hallway that was about 30 feet away. I saw them roll Mary in, and I said to myself, "Well, this is going to be really tremendous." I was excited sitting there.

All of a sudden, I heard a big scream, and I knew it was Mary screaming. I thought, "I don't care what the local laws are, what the regulations are, what I'm supposed to do, I'm going in there." So, I whipped into the delivery room as fast as I could.

The doctor was not even in the room yet. Mary had her legs up in the stirrups and said to the nurses, "You know what? I have this urge to push."

They said, "Oh, that's fine, you can push."

She pushes and Boom! Out the baby came and fell. That's when she screamed. She thought it was a pressure relief that she had pushed the baby right out but she didn't know if it was lying on the floor or not.

Meanwhile, I whipped into the delivery room in time to see that our baby was born sunny-side up. With the natural birth and the fact that a baby's head is soft and pliable, all that pushing turned my first son's head to a cone shape. The first time I saw my son, he looked straight up at me with a cone head as if to say, "Hey, how's everything going?"

Age 30 to 35

I was with Procter and Gamble. I was promoted twice in one day. When you work for P&G, you get promoted every couple of years, and you have to move. I was to transfer to the nearest corporate office in Jacksonville, Florida, and I was living in Tampa at that time.

I talked to P&G, and told them that I thought there should be uniformity, that people should stay where they are, instead of skipping all over the United States. I pointed out that I had all these great relationships in Tampa and that I would have to start over in Jacksonville. My recommendation was they should promote me twice and have me stay where I was. They said, "Okay," so I stayed.

At that same age, I had my second child and experienced that amazing miracle a second time. To think that we as human beings can create other human beings is really amazing.

Age 35 to 40

My third son was born as I was promoted again at Procter and Gamble. Again, I didn't have to move. I wanted to be part of a new restructure they had that, instead of managing a small geographic area, would make me responsible for a major account. It probably could be regarded as getting promoted twice again, but it was a brand new structure that they had created.

During that time, P&G was making changes to the new structure, and I had input. I told them I would be the most qualified to run these accounts and should be in essence a general manager. That took four or five months but it happened. It's amazing. You can be working with corporate conservatives and still get what you want. You have to have that will and desire to believe that it can happen to you and not pay any attention to any of the other things.

I was managing almost a billion-dollar business after that promotion. I expanded my imagination and thought about what I wanted, and I got it. I believed I was the best person for that job, and I got it.

Age 40 to 45

One of the best times, was when I became a golf member. I was a member of the country club because of my high position and high pay. I wasn't a golfer at all, but I loved being out in nature and I loved being with my children.

My children weren't at the country club to golf either, they were there for the golf cart. I would take my three boys and go out on the golf course. We would drive around to the different holes and see alligators, big beautiful birds and be out in nature.

We would play a little golf, have a marvelous time riding around in golf carts, and we would have a fun hitting the ball.

I would take my boys to Busch Gardens. There are different exhibits and animals to see, for all ages. Some areas had rides, like a little train, and all the kids had fun riding. We are, after all, really here to have fun in this world.

Busch Gardens had this one game we played. There was a tall milk can with a small opening on the top. You throw a softball, and if you have the right spin, you can land that softball in the hole. If you hit that, you got a huge stuffed animal.

Well, I knew exactly how to do it so we won this big stuffed animal, bigger than the kids were.

They were walking out of Busch Gardens, loving that their dad had won them a big stuffed animal. We had stuffed animals everywhere in our house because almost every time we went I won at least one.

Age 45 to 50

This was an interesting time in my life. I was going through seminary school. It was here that I experienced the highest stimulation of thoughts that I've ever had.

I decided to go to seminary school for a four-year program. I wanted to go there because I really didn't understand this God thing, and I wanted to learn more!

The highlight of those years was the realization that I can verbalize in other terms besides the Father, Son, and Holy Spirit. I understood how amazing each one of us is and what amazing creators we are, and how we can become deliberate creators, and have all that we want.

Age 50 to 55

This is around the time when my car accident occurred, and I really don't remember much—between the unbearable pain I was in, going to outpatient rehab, and the IV's in me.

As I began to write this section, I truly did not have any memories to draw out. So I said to myself and my Source, "I want to remember age 50 to 55. Please tell me an amazing thing that happened?" I asked for it and this is what came. If you continue to ask, it will be there.

This was an amazing time. I was losing my power to the insurance company and medical doctors and their drugs. I wanted to regain my power. I recognized one little thought the size of a mustard seed (so tiny that I barely recognized it): I needed to take back my power.

Faith born out of a mustard seed. That's what happened. It was recognizing that thought; it was me with a simple idea that I was losing my power and I had to regain it.

I knew I had to grab hold of this thought and regain my power because otherwise I would go under, be swarmed by them, and let them take over my power. I expanded that little mustard seed into creating what I am now and all that I have been afterwards.

That one strand of thought. That's all I needed.

Age 55 to 60

I really started to be aware of the magnificent creator that I am, and that all of us beings are. I started feeling truly empowered. The moment of my empowerment, where I felt so good and my heart sang, happened when I was in Tampa.

I felt I needed to go to a bigger city. I needed to start thriving. I moved to Dallas, Texas! The most memorable flight is me taking off, feeling the wheels lift off from the Tampa airport, and knowing that I was leaving. I knew this plane trip would lead me to a more abundant and happier life. That's exactly what happened, because I believed it would, and it did.

> *Amazing things happened here in Dallas that I could have never imagined I would create. I could never have come up with these cooperative components that the Source provides when I think about what I want and why I want it.*
>
> *Hundreds of people have done this exercise, and they were able to easily change their story. By changing your story, you start changing your thought process and you'll start thinking about more of what you want.*
>
> *Remember, it takes discipline. I know you can do it.*

Chapter 15

The Power of Thought and Mindfulness

God with a small "g" is the god that honors other people's opinions. I think the biggest gods with a small "g" are the doctors who think they do the healing. Doctors are wonderful, they can fix many problems, and they are valuable, but they don't do the healing.

We Have the Power to Overcome Anything

I created a training process called *Top Performers*. There are people who have used their power to overcome. They have overcome cancer. They have been in car accidents and suffered with chronic pain in their neck and healed themselves in no more than six weeks. They have healed from the things the doctor said such as, "Oh, you're going to be in chronic pain the rest of your life," or "You have cancer so we're going to have to do all these treatments."

Most of us don't believe in the Source power that is available to us, so we ignore it. We have so much power that lies in the six inches between our ears, and yet we turn away from it.

When nobody thought you could run a mile under four minutes, nobody did. However, after the first person accomplished this feat, suddenly more and more people ran less than a four-minute mile that same year. It was possible because now they could see it and believe it.

They said, "Oh, it must be true because I've seen it in physical form."

When you say, "Oh, this is true for me," it will happen. Whether anybody has ever done it before; whether this is a physical experience or not.

I boldly claim that if you're missing a limb, you could actually re-grow your limb, even though nobody has done that before. We just haven't experienced it or seen it, so there is no belief to support it. Expand your imagination beyond what people say is possible or beyond what other people have done before; you can do that.

I made up that I want to be promoted twice in one day, unheard of at Procter and Gamble. I did it. What that showed me returns to my empowerment and how each of us is empowered to create the things we want in our life. I don't care how the stock market is doing or whatever the situation may be, you can create beyond what is commonly perceived as possible.

Another example is Stephen Curry. This basketball player is amazing at making a three-point shot. The other day, I saw a seven-year-old kid who did this amazing dribble like "Steph" Curry, and shot a three-pointer on a regular court and everything.

This kid is seven years old! What I'm telling you is this: if he hadn't seen "Steph" Curry do that before, that child might never have done that.

Understand that when we go "beyond" in our imagination, we uplift the world. Whatever you do, whether you smile or you frown, it is going impact the world in some way.

Something for you to think about.

We Have the Power to Be Happy

How can I be happy? When I'm happy, I can uplift others. We are leaders when we do something that nobody else has done. When we achieve what it is that we want to do, we then give other people inspiration to do the same. We don't realize the rippling effect that we have on the world. The most wonderful thing you can do is to stand tall and decide what you do want, ask for it, and receive it.

I went to seminary school because I had this feeling of the presence of God, but I didn't fully understand it. I felt this feeling when I held the bayonet to my chest, and the gun to my head. I felt the presence of something that was there, but I didn't have it figured out. I felt that if maybe I went to seminary school, I would figure it out.

My "ah-ha" moment in seminary school was when they drew a large circle. Then, the cut the circle from top to bottom in three parts.

The top part is the Father. The Divine Self.

The Father is at the top, the Divine Self, and we are each divine. We can reach to our divine self, our higher self, that taps into the mind of God, the mind of our Source. That's the Father. That's where it can all start. That's where we want our Source to get our thoughts, to receive and tap into these Godly thoughts.

The Holy Spirit is in the middle of that circle.

The Holy Spirit is all that is. Or, another way to look at that, the Law of Attraction. Whatever you're thinking (your divine thoughts), that is the energy that creates the world. We can create with our thoughts. Our thoughts will bring similar components, cooperative components—things, places, people, to us. These things will bring our divine thoughts to us.

Then the Son, the experience, is at the bottom of the circle.

For us to experience this on earth, and for us to manifest these divine thoughts using all of these, the Law of Attraction takes those thoughts and turns the energy into things.

When I saw this simple diagram, I realized that I don't need to go to divinity school. I realized that this was the answer that I wanted. I understood. In fact, scientists have quantum physics, and molecular biologists have agreed in the last five years that this is how creation happens.

The Father. The Divine Self

The Holy Spirit

The Son. The Experience

This is how matter is formed, and it all starts with our thoughts according to the scientists. That is the power in each one of us.

We Have the Power to Create with Thought

We're lazy with our thoughts. We're real concerned about how we dress, how we look, all these things. But we are lax with how we think. For the most part, we are undisciplined when it comes to thinking about what we want.

If I continue to look at what's happening and continue to give it my thought, I'll continue to have the same experience because my thought creates the matter. I'll continue to experience the same thing. It might be the same bad relationship, and if I continue to think of that person as bad, I'll continue to create that.

According to the scientists:

Step One: Begin with your thought

You have to know what you want. Thought creates energy. The way that we would look at it is, thought creates emotion. The emotions are the energy.

Step Two: Focus your thought to send a signal (energy)

If for one minute you focus your thoughts on a certain subject, you start sending out a signal. That energy signals Source. This energy is answered and immediately returned by Source.

Step Three: Energy creates matter

The energy creates matter. That's our experience. It's the same thought that I was given in seminary school, about how this divine mind of ours works. To tap into it all we have to do is ask.

Tap into this divinity to get these beautiful abundant thoughts, they will start streaming to you, and they will light up your emotions. Your emotions send the signal and Source answers and receives it in energy form. Then all we have to do is to allow it in to experience it in our life.

Some people get impatient and think, "I have the thought, I have the energy, so where's my stuff?" That's what they ask.

When you ask, "Where's my stuff?" you are sending mixed messages again. You're making sure it doesn't come to you. Know that your stuff is already here in energy form. Allow it to be. It just hasn't materialized in a form that you can see. Feel it and know that it is coming into your experience. As you think upon that, it will happen, and you will have your dreams come true. You will be the happiest person in the world, too!

The Voice of God

One night many years ago, I was on my private plane with only the pilot and myself. I was listening to *Conversations with God* by Neale Donald Walsch. I loved the audio. It's a great book. There was a moment where he said that life was upsetting, he didn't have enough money and his relationships were not good; things were not working out so well. He returns home and finds all of his furniture is missing. "Oh, my God!" he said. "I've been robbed. This is terrible."

In his bedroom he found his bed and his clothes. He hadn't been robbed; his wife and children had left him.

At that point, he really got upset and said, "God, I am pissed off, if you really are there, you better start talking to me."

All of a sudden, he heard an energy vibration that came to him, and he started to have thoughts. He was determined, "God are you really there?"

And God answered, "What do you want?" That was the beginning of Conversations with God.

Well, I'm taking off in this plane at night. As we were going through the clouds, I'm listening to the book Conversations with God and God is talking. On the audio book, He has the male voice of God that most people would think.

Suddenly, as we're going through the clouds, I notice the whole sky lights up. The beautiful stars and full moon are shining brightly. Just then the voice of God switched to a female voice. It was like everything came together for me. Male. Female. It made no difference. There are physical differences, yes. But we're all in this together. We're all connected with this cord of love and hope, and for us to love each other and to recognize that there is no competition. There is only good and only love, and when you see through the eyes of God, through Source or as some would say through the eyes of Christ, we are all the same.

When you recognize this, you shall see this beautiful world and all the beautiful people in it and how deeply we are all tied together in this beautiful place that we call "the world."

Awaken Your Consciousness

To look at my last couple of years, becoming enlightened to this amazing world and knowing how life plays and how I can have life play for me, has been an empowering and joyful experience. I'm at the point where I tap into creative intelligence and creative intelligence helps me.

I'm asking God to awaken my consciousness for me.

I'm committed to developing even more vision and to unify this beautiful world, to call forth more faith for me, to help the world evolve into the better, more loving place that it is and can be.

I ask to deepen my intuition and harmonize myself with *all that is* to achieve liberation and experience more freedom. That's what we are here for—to have more freedom, more joy, and to embrace the high ideals and the greatness of this world and to tap into those beings both higher and more enlightening.

I'm calling for light to come into my body and give me heightened divine thoughts that are available to all of us for our choosing. They can come to us and create divinity in form. It is divine thoughts that I want to put into form to be an example to others.

The most effective way that I can teach is through example.

For me to continue to tap into this, and to enjoy this beautiful divine world, I have to create an inner world as well. As I do that, everything comes from the inner world.

I know that I can be the master, that I am to manifest the things that I want, and it's all coming to me. Some people would call that patience. Know that when you ask, there's a bit of a delay in receiving it. It could be a minute or it could be a year. But there's a delay.

Know though, that you have a concierge working on your behalf. Everything is working together for you so that it's a joyful experience for you. You'll be skipping along knowing that all those things you've asked for are on their way. They're here right now like every new conversation, every new thought, and it's all guiding you towards what you want by your good feelings.

As long as you are being guided and following those good thoughts, everything you have wanted will be delivered.

> *Each of us has the power to change and improve our thinking to more positive thoughts. It amazes me how many people, before I coach them, are fighting for their lack and limitation.*

> *The easiest way is to take one step forward.*

Tell me something good that has happened in the last 24 hours. What good things happened for you? As you start looking for that, God is going to help you.

See, the beauty is that we always have the Source that will lead us to whatever we're asking for. Let Source know, "I want to improve my thinking." "I want to think more about what I want," and you shall.

If you really can't think of anything, keep asking yourself, "What's one thing that happened that was good in my entire lifetime?" You will have an answer. Start there. Take one step forward.

Focus on that. I promise you within a minute, you'll start that energy flowing. Your Source will start to answer you. You'll find another good thing and another good thing.

Chapter 16

The Joy Shop

No matter whether your morning is 5 am or 11 am or 7 pm, begin your day with joy. Every morning, invest 15 minutes in yourself before you begin the hustle of the day. Maybe after your shower, maybe as you enjoy the first cup of coffee. Use *15 Minutes to My Happiness and Joy* as a guide and tool to change your thinking from negative to positive.

Change it up. Personalize it. Whatever it takes, read it every day. This will attract good feeling thoughts that will automatically raise your vibration, raising your point of attraction.

Fifteen Minutes to My Happiness & Joy!!!

I begin this fabulous day by breathing in deeply as I ask to be led by My Heart today!

I refresh and renew Myself as I lift My Vibration to that of High Flying Energy that leverages the Power that creates worlds and sends the signal of My desires!

All People, events and things are cooperative components to My desires today... what fun and how easy is this!

I am becoming healthier, wealthier, happier, younger, stronger, wiser, and more prosperous every day in every way!

I love how I invest this all powerful present moment to pre-pave and make My day the best day ever!

I practice the thoughts of My desires today!

I now lead and am led by Heart! I am flowing My way with joy to My desires!

I reach others by being who I am! As I blend My Heart and Mind, I manifest as a Master!

I am enough! I am worthy! I am raising My feelings to all My desires!

I have convinced Myself of the Creator that I am!

I have come into an emotional space of feeling good with high flying vibration! I have come into a place of knowing how Life works!

I take credit for My Life... all of it! I have struck it rich!

The larger part of Me holds My desires, and I go there now!

I have come to a point of clarity of Me and My Life! I am now enjoying My Life!

I turn My vibration to where it feels better and feels right!

I trust the Stream of Abundance and I am being guided by Heart.

My business is now thriving as I focus on the clients I want and on the Ideal Referral Partnerships that bring Me My Ideal Clients.

I love allowing $_____ or more into My checking account each month.

All and everything are now Cooperative Components to Me and My Desires and I now allow all to act on My behalf!

I am now uplifted and allow to be led by Heart! I trust in My knowing!

I am now clear, aligned, and embracing My Present Moment and being led by Heart!

The perfect thoughts, feelings, words, body language, and Energy Vibration now flow to Me easily and powerfully today!

I look for evidence of being blessed and being delivered My desires. I allow more of the essence of who I am to rise like a cork in My Life!

I dance with Life and with this magnificent day that brings me Joy! I allow the essence of who I am to be guided today.

I love that I am always surrounded by cooperative components of My thoughts.

I love how I am allowing My cells to be their natural and healthy selves!

I love being healthy, youthful, good looking, inspiring, uplifting, charming, and a fun person.

I lighten up and enjoy this wonderful day! I come from Heart.

I make things happen with the Power of My Heart & Mind!

I am backed by an almighty Loving Power that is present with me now!

Well-being is my core and I go there now. Today I offer a fresh and high vibration! I have decided to enjoy My Life!

I expect miracles to happen to, for, and with Me today!

Today is the best day I have ever had and My desires flow naturally and powerfully to me! I am the Master Heart & Mind of My Manifestations!

I appreciate all that I have, all that I am, all that I am becoming, and all that I co-create today!

I now relax and enjoy this day unfolding perfectly and powerfully for Me!

I am a Cooperative Component to All That Is, all during this awesome day!

I appreciate My Source leading Me and how I adore this Present Moment!

I love You, Eternally Me!!!!!!!!!!!!!!!!!!!!!!!!!!

After you are done reading these powerful, divine words, you will be in a position to start attracting what you want to you. That is when you take the next 3 steps that will make your day even more fabulous!

Invest another 10 to 15 minutes and write down three things:

Step One: What is it that I Want?

Ask for what you want. Something simple to begin with, perhaps "I want to have a long, healthy happy and prosperous life." Don't we all want that? Absolutely! So start out nice and general, nice and easy.

Here's what mine looks like: I want my travels to flow smoothly and easily. (Instead of, I don't want to have bad traffic.) I want wonderful, deep, and meaningful relationships. I want to laugh more today. I want to enjoy more today. I want to savor more today. I want to look and feel younger every day. (I always giggle on this one when I do *The Joy Shop*. But really, if you have that feeling of youthfulness, you'll start to look more youthful.)

Start writing down the things that you want. No need to limit the number of things you ask for.

Step Two: What Do You Appreciate in the Past 24 Hours?

We have been disciplined to look at and to focus on the bad in our life. Turn on the news and they hunt the world over to report bad when there are billions of great things that happened in the world at that same time. Our undisciplined mind works much the same way.

Looking for the negative is like putting gas on the fire. Stop all that because it's going to give you more of what you don't want.

Instead change your thinking process by looking at the last 24 hours. Find what played out for you; honor what you appreciate. Then it becomes simple. This doesn't have to be huge. It could be a stranger smiled at you. Cherish that and enjoy it. A friend gave you a nice comment. Your travels were smooth and easy and even fun. You feel better. You woke up this morning with your heart beating.

When you start looking for things that are playing out for you that you appreciate, it's endless. The beauty of appreciation is that when you talk about what you appreciate, you automatically tell God, "I want more of it!"

> *You could use Gratitude instead of Appreciation. I think that calling this being in a state of appreciation is really a better word than grateful because grateful is being thankful for what somebody else did. The fact is that you and Source did it so I appreciate it. You're telling yourself that I appreciate us creating this because we create everything in the world.*

"Well hold on," some people will say, "you didn't create that car accident, Dr. Hank."

Well, yes I did. I was unhappy in my life, and I needed a way out. Now, there would have been an easier way out, but you know that didn't happen. We talked about this in Chapter 9.

Think *Yellow* when you ask for what you want. Think *Red* when, during the day you think about what you don't want. And you get orange in your experience when you mix the two, muddling not only your thoughts but what you create as well.

So my car accident was an orange. It's not what I really wanted, but it's what I was asking for because I was not focused precisely on the yellow.

To finish Step 2, write down what you appreciate and what played out for you in the last 24 hours.

Step Three: Now, Pre-pave Your Day!

Most people aren't deliberate in creating their life, and that's what we are doing in Step 3. Write how you want your day to go.

> *Here's how mine might start out: Yes. My travels are going to be smooth and easy. The meeting is going to be delightful.*
>
> *Don't get too specific like buying a million-dollar house or whatever the thing is. Keep it simple like we'll get a long break together, that we enjoy each other, we have a fun time. Keep it easy, keep it simple and you'll see as you keep it on the wanted side, you'll get more than you had asked for and your cup overflows. The key is simple: Ask. We are the creators of our experience; we are deliberate creators.*

As you make *The Joy Shop* a habit and write out the three steps, you will quickly see results. It will start getting a little better and a little better and a little better. You have to have patience. You know it's all coming because your Source, all your angels, are busy at work, gathering all the goodies and everything that you want, and it's all coming to you.

Ninety-nine percent of what we create is in our thoughts and then the 1% is our inspired actions that we get from our alignment with our Source. Our Source will give us thoughts of inspired actions and we will then take these actions.

We have been told, "We have to work hard. It's a struggle out there." That simply is not true. You don't know what is going to happen next. All you have to do is focus. As you focus, all of your dreams will come true by doing that.

CHAPTER 17

Top Performers

Twenty years ago I created a training process, *Top Producers*, that has been used successfully within Corporate America and by select individuals and entrepreneurs. It takes about five weeks to complete and immediately you can start manifesting virtually anything you want, including specific measurable results; more income, better health, whatever you set your mind on.

It all started when I was with Procter and Gamble.

They had me on a fast track. Half of the time I was developing the business, half of the time I was in training and development. I received all this amazing, incredible information and understanding about how business really works. I was in about year 14 with them, and I was managing the Southeast United States, about a billion-dollar business.

Our patents started to run out, and we were losing market share to private label. This put us in a situation where we really didn't know what to do. So, I started thinking, "How can we improve our market share? They have a better price, but not a better product than ours."

Based on my understanding as a mental scientist, I understood that our thought creates everything. I thought, "Well, why not use what I know personally with big business?"

I created *Top Performers* and had about 175 of my team go through this process. At the time, it was seven weeks long. (It has since been improved, and it only takes five weeks.)

Every week, we would meet for two hours. Our specific objective on the professional side was to increase our sales. It would increase our profit and thus increase our market share. We had that focus on the professional side. The process also included the tools that I provide to focus on something in their personal life.

What I had found in my past business experience is that sometimes people were, for example, having marital problems. Even though they would show up at work, they really didn't show up for work. They were too concerned about what was going on at home to be good in their business life.

I felt that it was one of the keys to the success process to include the personal goals. The personal stuff isn't shared necessarily with all the members of the group. We had natural work teams. I was not putting 175 people in one room; typically, it was only eight to 12 people, the manager and their team. Their objective was to increase sales specifically on whatever they could impact. I was responsible for all functions and divisions at Procter and Gamble other than manufacturing.

We offered technology expertise, customer service at store level, and developed the best place where the products should be on the shelf for enhanced sales and profits. There were a lot of disciplines that were involved in this. They each had their own professional goal. But then, they also identified their personal goal.

The results were outstanding!

The net result is that our revenues increased by 21% and our cost decreased by 34%. We were hitting it out of the park when most of the United States was basically flat in both of those areas where we were showing tremendous gains.

When I started to see these results, I decided to leave Procter and Gamble. I realized I loved helping people to become their greatest possibility. I loved helping them to achieve measurable business results and equal success in their personal lives. It really made my heart sing. I realized this was my passion.

What is your passion?

That is for all of us to hang our hat on. Whatever you love to do, do it! Don't shoot it down. We shoot ourselves in the foot a lot of times. We start thinking, "Oh well, how will I get business? How will that work?" We keep getting engaged in the "how," and that's not our business. That's God's business to figure out the "how."

Despite the fact that I had all of these corporate trainings (P&G is the largest advertiser in the world), I didn't really know how to market myself if I went out on my own as a personal consultant. I could have easily shot myself in the foot by saying, "Well, I don't know how to market. How is this going to work?"

Instead, I allowed and trusted that God would show me the way. When I made the decision to leave Procter and Gamble, I had the opinions of others who told me not to do it. I had my in-laws saying, "Oh my God, you'll lose all that high income every year, all of those benefits, and your health benefits." They went on and on about all the reasons as to why I shouldn't leave the safety and comfort of P&G. My wife didn't want me to do it.

I decided that I was no longer going to honor the god (the little 'g' god) of other people's opinions. We all experience it, when we believe other people know best about what we should do, what direction we should go. They have good intentions, but the only person who knows what's best for you is you.

You know what's best for you when you think of an idea. I thought about leaving P&G to start my own consulting business to help people become their greatest possibility and help businesses measurably grow because I realized that money wasn't a bad or awful thing; it's an awesome thing.

By having money, you have more freedom, more choices. It was valuable, showing your own value to other people. If you want to help out the people who profit, this is one of the ways to do it.

A great example is democracy in the United States and what that has done to better the entire world. There are fewer people in poverty. There are more people moving into the middle class. We are improving all around the world. For us to embrace this idea about what other people think, really doesn't have anything to do with us.

It has to do with what you're thinking.

Pay attention to when you're feeling good about whatever you're thinking. You know that you are now doing things with the big 'G' God. You start identifying with what you want to do. I simply identified with what I wanted to do and did that. I felt great about it. Then, I trusted that God would show me the "how."

When I left P&G, who was my first client? Procter and Gamble! Funny how they were some of the other people telling me, "Don't leave. We want you to do this all around the country, around the world for us."

I said, "No, I'm leaving Procter and Gamble."

Nobody was in support of my leaving P&G with all that security. No one other than God and me, and that's all we ever need. It's between God and you to make your dreams come true.

I was in a position at P&G where I had clients such as IBM and Chase Bank. I had a lot of these different connections to Corporate America.

Despite the fact that I didn't know how to go out and market my services, and I didn't have millions of dollars for TV ads, I built a multibillion-dollar business using my process of creating referral partnerships. Those partnerships can be within a big company; they can be internal company's customers or external customers. Most people, especially entrepreneurs, will be external customers.

I developed from there. I developed a unique process to identify and formalize referral partners. I had clients at Chase, IBM, John Deere, and many, many others. The list is long and the measurable results are long. Chase initially invested $100,000 with me, and in less than six months they received $1.2 million back in increased profits.

In fact, the process is so time proven and solid, that I guaranteed at least a 400% return on their investment or the investment was returned in full. I was really blessed to get into all these wonderful large clients.

I now use this with other markets, such as the real estate industry, where we've had amazing results. Real estate agents who are selling one home every other month, will go to selling four homes a month.

And, it works in their personal lives, too! I had a client who, like me, was in a car accident resulting in chronic pain. He was going to the doctors and chiropractors every week. His time was consumed in going to different people who were giving their opinion on how to heal him. They told him he would have chronic pain for the rest of his life. Then he went through *Top Performers*. Within three weeks he started to feel better because his goal was to improve his health. He stopped focusing on his pain and guess what? He started noticing less pain. (Funny how that works!)

Eventually, he stopped going to the doctors, in much the same way that I did. He has perfect health now. The *Top Performers* process can help anybody. What the process does is help people to be mentally focused on the things that they want and that leads them to achieve anything.

What's really great is when people get engaged. Sometimes people are concerned; a lot of employees are disengaged with Corporate America because they fear being laid off. They don't feel important.

This process works because it gets people engaged in at least their personal life. Their increased engagement starts spilling over into their professional life. It takes disengaged employees and helps them become engaged and loyal because of the company's decision to use this process. It then helps them to move forward more empowered. Corporate loyalty grows because employees are saying, "I really appreciate how my company helped me with my personal life and because of that, I'll give back."

It Starts at the Top

Typically, *Top Performers* starts at the top. I have worked with the entire executive team. I begin by asking the CEO or the owner, "What measurable results do you want?"

Usually their response isn't really a measurable result that they want. For example, they'll say, "I want my people more productive." That's not measurable.

I'll say, "Okay, I understand that. But, when they get more productive, what do you get out of that?"

I use focused practice to get down to the nut of what they want, usually increased sales or better customer experience. And, it's not unusual for the CEO, President or top executive to say, "Oh it's 'these' people who have the problem." They are pointing to some department.

Typically, like in any organization, what happens in Corporate America starts at the top and then runs down. I work with the Executive Management Team first, and in every case they will have significant, measurable results.

Top Performers is tailored to each company.

Instead of meeting once a week for a couple of hours, maybe we only need to meet once a month; some processes and new ideas take longer than a week. For example, a warehouse decided to shift around products so they could be more efficient in getting products shipped out in a timelier manner. That could not be done in a week, so we followed up in a month.

I work with upper management looking at which area(s) need change. One of the areas is always sales. That is one of our specialties and is measured specific to the company's goals. It is managed in every facilitation and during every week.

The information here is conveyed in a way to address these specific goals so it's unique. In addition to the specific goal, it is also defined with each person within that area. If you're dealing with management, there's a section for management.

If you're dealing with sales, there is an assessment that is done to show the six steps of the sales process, and it helps the individual understand where they're at vs. what the six steps are. Most people don't even know what the six steps of the sales process are.

It's invaluable information.

It's typically upper management, management, sales, and customer service that are the focal points. In fact, at Chase, one of their main goals was to increase their level of customer service. That's where with a $100,000 investment, over $1.2 million worth of cost savings and efficiencies were recovered within only four months.

Success Units

Where is the magic? Some people say all that sounds really good, but how do you do it?

In the last five years, neuroscientists, quantum physicists and molecular biologists, all the major disciplines of science, have agreed on how creation is created. How is it made? Based on the scientists and what I've been teaching for over 20 years, it all starts here.

There are five Success Units that outline the process. I'll share within each Success Unit how it the magic happens, how it's done.

Thought Success Unit

It's really a five-step process of creation. The first step is to start with our thought and different areas of thoughts. Those thoughts create a signal. Those signals are the emotions. That signal is then sent to our Source, to the Universe. This energy (you have to have this) takes about a minute to get going. You send out this signal and instantly Source answers and responds to your core request, to your prayer, which is thought.

We want in the first Success Unit to understand the power that we have and where our thoughts are.

Step One

Begin with the power of thought. Everything comes from our thought. The scientists state that thought creates energy. For us humans, instead of putting it in a scientific term, energy is simply our emotions. With our thoughts, we create this energy, which is our emotions.

Step Two

Create our energy (emotions) into a signal to Source. That signal begins to create the process of energy becoming matter.

Step Three

Create matter (according to the terminology of the scientist). Matter is our physical experience. The scientists almost have it right, they forgot to include God in this. Like, the doctors for example, they don't do the healing even though many of them think they do. How do you get from God what you ask for? How do you manifest it?

Step Four

Manifesting is a beautifully defined thing that each one of us has the ability to do. We can manifest into this world the things that we think about. Step 4 is about allowing this energy in and giving it enough time to manifest.

I call it ABE (allow, believe and expect).

Often we say, "Well I want this," but it doesn't happen soon enough so we start thinking, "Well, where is it? Why isn't it here, it must not work."

Or, "God, I would really like to have more business," when we are praying on our hands and knees in the morning.

However, during the day our prayers are at every moment, "Oh, I don't have enough business. Why isn't more business coming in?"

That gets us back to the yellow thoughts mixed with red thoughts to manifest orange matter. And, we didn't want orange matter, but we aren't aware that we are mixing up our signal to Source with all kinds of interference.

Stay the course and trust that whatever you have asked for is on its way to you.

Step Five

Bring it into our existence. Source loves us and is compassionate and interested in us. Source is involved within us and wants to give us everything.

The greatest thing for our Source to do is to provide us what we ask for. It's like our children, we want to give to all of our children.

Source wants to give to you when you are open to receiving it!

That is creation.

The Zones Success Unit

There are four zones in which we can find ourselves living. Three are Red Zones and one is the Green Zone. The Green Zone is the optimum place to live your life. It's about living deliberately.

One of the Red Zones is Busy Work

When we find ourselves doing non-important things and doing them urgently, this is busy work, and it places us in a Red Zone. For example, Saturday morning you awaken and have coffee, read the paper, then turn on the TV, and before you know it, your objectives have been untouched. Your stress increases.

At work, you are interrupted when someone asks you to do so something for them. Your email box is filled with one request after the next, you receive too many phone calls.

You find that your day is consumed by busy work leaving no room to conncct to your Higher Self. Little is achieved that will help you to become more successful. It looks like you are productive, but you focused on things that don't really matter to you or the Universe.

One of the Red Zones is Being Reactive

This is where we get life by default. We walk outside, we go to the meeting. We get whatever we get. We aren't creating anything; we are simply responding.

> *I will give you a fun little example. I'm a parachutist, and I jump out of the plane and all of a sudden I realize, "Oh what I want is a parachute that I forgot." It becomes too late to manifest; you're going to have to hang on. Good luck.*

That's the road. That's how most of us are in our lives. We are not deliberate. Then at the last moment we're in a meeting and we're thinking, "Oh, this isn't going good, and I want this to go well."

You are already in this negative momentum of what you don't want that is gaining even more momentum, and you can't stop it. It is the Law of Attraction in motion.

Of course, we all have the power to change things instantly even though most people don't believe that power exists. Thus, it doesn't happen to most people.

Normally when we are in this situation, let's say a bad meeting, a bad conversation is going on, we say, "I wish this would be a good conversation." Really what we are thinking is, "This isn't a good conversation."

God doesn't know English or Spanish or whatever language you speak. God only knows your emotions that you are sending out.

If you're sending out bad emotions, "It's not working well, but I'd like it to work," you immediately focus on that. It puts you in the focus point of, "This meeting didn't work well, or this conversation didn't work well." Thus, we get life by default.

Most people wake up in the morning and say, "God, I hope this happens and I hope that happens." As the day goes on, they get consumed with what is happening right now in their life, versus thinking about how they wanted it to be.

A great question we ask in *Top Performers* is "What do I want to do next?" It changes your mindset immediately. It changes your thought process from being reactive to now being deliberate and intentional. You get into your car you ask yourself, "What do I want next?"

You will start being answered not by your concrete physical mind, but by your divine mind. The answers will start to flow to you. "What do I want next? Wow! I want my travels to be smooth and easy and even fun. I want to arrive early."

We don't say, "Oh, I don't want any of that rush hour. I don't want any more of that traffic." When you say your travels are smooth and easy, you will start seeing that your travels become smooth and easy. We control the outside world, but we have been conditioned that we think we don't.

To be deliberate, ask yourself before walking into that meeting, "What do I want next?" Then visually and emotionally create that before you walk in.

It could be something like, I want an amazing meeting where everybody feels tremendous. We get along well. We laugh more, we smile, we enjoy ourselves, and we have harmony with each other.

When we keep it nice and general instead of, "I want to close this fifteen-million-dollar deal," and we allow Source to guide us to the perfect thoughts, words, body language, and tone of voice that will give us everything that we want to make that meeting go better than we ever could have imagined.

That's creating momentum, too. You want to say, "What kind of momentum am I creating in my life here?" You can change your momentum. How many of us say to ourselves, "It can't get any worse than this," and then it does?

Well, that's because we ask for it, because we were thinking "worse than this." The Universe doesn't understand I don't want this. When you state it, you are creating that emotion and you are going to get more of it.

For you to start taking control of our lives, imagine you have a whole symphony in front of you. You have this magic wand and you raise it up while the entire symphony can hardly wait to start stringing and playing its first notes when you take that first motion.

That magic wand is your thoughts.

That's how wonderful you are. You raise that magic wand and the Universe starts to play for you. What music are you going to play?

Too often, we play songs about the things that we fear.

One of the Red Zones is *the Committee*

This is a Red Zone where we are thinking about what we don't want, and we are being deliberate in it. Imagine in your mind, here is this beautiful mahogany table in a beautiful high ceiling office with executive chairs all around it. There are characters sitting in these executive chairs, and we have created the power of what I call The Committee.

In our own mind, The Committee has players. The player sitting to your left in the executive chair is Fear. (Fear is actually an acronym: False Evidence Appearing Real.) Some of the other players at the table are Worry, Doubt, Disbelief, Complaining, and Blaming.

Point one finger at somebody and look how many fingers are pointing back at you because it's all about you. You live in the middle of the Universe, your Universe. You call forth all the energy based on your thoughts. You have the ability to mold the energy with your thoughts. We have worry, doubt, complaining (Religions have done a good job in adding shame and guilt to The Committee).

All those committee members keep you away from who you really are. There is nothing to be shameful for, nothing to be guilty about. Whatever you think you have done is only considered bad because you have been told that it is bad; you have disbelief.

The fact is, it took you to this moment where you are reading this book, and you are starting to awaken and realize, "My God, I have these beliefs that no longer serve me." I had these committee members of fear, worry, doubt, complaining, blaming, shame, and guilt all in my head. They are not working on my behalf at all.

In fact, they have put me in a place that is killing me.

The Committee kills us, often with stress. We all have committee members. Which ones we have and how strong they are depends on us, the individual.

How many of us have sat up in the middle of the night, not sleeping because we are worried about something? We toss and turn. That's The Committee keeping you up. The next day you're tired and you're not clear on what you want. It gets worse.

You are experiencing this process, allowing me to share with you knowledge of what is going on. In a snap of the fingers now, start getting better by releasing The Committee.

Do not pay any attention to committee members. Instead live in the Green Zone.

The Green Zone is Living Deliberately

In the Green Zone you think about exactly what you want, and you do it deliberately. This Green Zone increases success and empowers every area of your life. The Green Zone decreases stress because you are bending to God's will.

> *I am living in the Green Zone. I am living the life of my soul. I am being the deliberate creator of the things that make me feel good.*
>
> *You should consider doing the same.*

Why are you the deliberate creator of only the things that make you feel good? Because when you think about things that make you feel good, that feeling of good comes from your Source, telling you that you are thinking as your Source, as God thinks. Thus it aligns with your Source and places you on your lighted path. That success bursts you into your lighted path where you are skipping along, whistling, and happy.

The angels play their harps and sing.

The chimes you hear are the joyful sounds of the Universe.

Birth the ideas you want. Then ask for those ideas to come to fruition. It's like having low hanging fruit come right into your existence.

Diagnostic Tests

We have diagnostic tools that measure the stress you have in your life. Using these tools increases your health by understanding your stress. We teach you how to modify your behavior so that you can have less stress.

It's an incredible process and assessment that helps people to better understand themselves and others and will improve their business, their relationships, their personal lives, and their personal relationships.

It is an online assessment and takes about 15 minutes to complete. It includes a complete assessment on your behaviors and provides a 52-page recap of your behaviors. In the report will be a graph of who you really are and a second a graph showing you how you might modify your behavior to decrease stress.

The report outlines six different motivators and has pages discussing each one of those motivators.

It shows you exactly where your motivations are and where you rank with the average person. You get to know the mean as well as the category into which 68% the population falls.

If you score low or high that's neither good nor bad. If you score low in the motivators, you may have a difficult time speaking the language of people who are higher in that particular motivation or vice versa.

If you are really high, you embrace this motivation so much that you don't understand why other people don't think this way and make decisions this way. Being so strong in one type of motivation can get in the way of your relationships. Again, not good or bad.

The Six Motivators

This assessment gives you an understanding on how the world is actually valued by you specifically. You can look at the mean and recognize there are six ways that people value the world. Then look at the world and you can understand how they value it by the questions they are asking. By listening to what they are saying you can pick up these values, and you can start speaking their language because all of us have a curtain that we either draw down or raise up.

Haven't you met a person where all of a sudden, you can't figure out why you don't like this person? You can't wait to get out of there. You put your curtain down; you close them out. There is a way to raise the curtain of communication with everybody.

Think of the progress and the deep meaningful relationships that you are offering. You can get more people saying, "Yes," to you instead of a closed curtain.

It helps when dealing with people to understand that people are motivated and make decisions in different ways than you do. There are six different ways that people are motivated.

The assessment measures your motivations, and how you make decisions based on these six factors. It's useful to understand what motivates you and what motivates others. Once you understand how other people are motivated, you can start talking their language, instead of talking your own language.

Utilitarian Motivation

These are people who make decisions based on a return on their investment (money, time, energy, and resources). They want the facts and figures.

Social Motivation

These are people who make decisions based on how it is going to help people.

Theoretical Motivation

These are people who make decisions based on knowledge. They need lots and lots of knowledge before they are comfortable to make a decision.

Individualistic Motivation

These are people who make decisions based on wanting to be the best. They want the biggest and best of everything. The want to be Number One.

Traditional Motivation

These are people who make decisions that keep with how they currently do things. They wake up at the same time, do their job the same way. They like rules and regulations and keeping everything uniform.

Aesthetic Motivation

These are people who make decisions based on form and harmony. They want to grow and evolve and experience the moment.

Examples

Let me give you a few examples of how this works so you can begin to improve how you communicate with others who are different from you.

If I am a high Utilitarian Motivator and I start talking to someone and say, "Look at the great return you have…" and they are not Utilitarian Motivation; what I say won't motivate them.

Let's say they are high Social Motivation which means they like helping other people. If you are talking about return on investment and what makes them more money, they won't listen.

Instead, speak their language and talk about how what you are doing will help other people. If they know your project is helping others, right away they would say, "Yes!" If you are talking about what they get out of it financially, you are not speaking their language, so they'll probably lose interest.

Speaking someone's language starts building deep and meaningful relationships, whether it's internal customers, external customers, or within your family. It starts enhancing your life experience with people, and most of your goals are going to be achieved. It starts with you asking for what you want in their language, not yours.

You are going to attract the people who will have the means to give you whatever you are asking for, just make sure you understand that it may come in other "languages."

Here's another great example of how to speak with people. Recently I had a coaching client who told me, "Oh, you know John Doe wanted the biggest house in the neighborhood, and I talked him out of it."

I said, "Why did you do that?"

He said, "It was not good for him because he didn't have a good return on his investment."

I said, "But, I can guarantee you that he wanted the biggest home in the neighborhood."

There are people out there (Individualistic Motivation) who want to be the best, to have the best and biggest house in the neighborhood. They really don't care if they can't sell their house for as much money per square foot versus other houses in the neighborhood, because they are so much bigger than the other homes that are in the neighborhood. Typically, you don't get a good return on your investment.

This agent truly thought he did this client a favor, but he did not. What really motivated them and what they valued is that they wanted to have the biggest house. They laughed at that real estate agent and went to another real estate agent, who helped them buy the biggest house in another neighborhood.

Of course, it was well intentioned. However, he was stuck in the way he valued the world thinking that is the way everyone else values the world.

If you are real high social, you sometimes help other people despite yourself. An example of that is, mom's cooking dinner, and the neighbor knocks on the door and says, "Oh, can you help me. I need to have someone to watch my baby right now."

She automatically says, "Oh yeah, let me take the baby." When she comes back, the food is burnt because she forgot about her dinner.

There are people (you know who you are) who continue to help others so much that it takes away from their experience. When you take away from your experience, then you are no longer thriving, even though all the people around you are thriving.

The value for aesthetic people is to enjoy the moment. They want to get into the moment, so they can experience it. When you're speaking to them, you're engaging them into the experience that you're having and to the experience of what you're sharing with them, that way they can really get into the moment.

Using Assessments for Hiring

I'm often hired to recruit for larger companies based on these assessments. I don't even have to meet the candidate in person, and I can easily pick the best person for the job. This whole hiring process overall increases retention by 50% for companies saving them lots of time and money. It increases productivity by 30% versus the normal way of using the resume and the interview process, which is an unreliable process.

First, I'll do a benchmark of the job for which we are hiring. I determine out of these six motivators, which are the most important for this job. For example, if it's a commission position, it's probably Utilitarian Motivation, a return on investment would be number one motivator. We want those people to be motivated by the job.

Then I measure the individuals and find out how they are motivated. If they are not high Utilitarian Motivation, I'm not going to hire them, because they are not motivated by commission, so they are not going to do a good job for me. It's truly a magical way for me to employ the right people for each particular job.

Then the assessment goes into the behavior styles. Hippocrates in 300 B.C. identified four different behavior styles. In a whole exercise within 30 seconds, I will identify the behavior style of any individual. Then I'll modify your behavior style so you can more effectively open that window of communication.

That is a broad view of understanding yourself and others. It is also an incredible process for understanding motivation because most people don't have a clue. There are few people in the world that measure or have the diagnostic tools to measure that.

I have the world's most statistically accurate and valid diagnostic tool that measures not only their behavior and their motivators, but also their talents. It measures to the tenth of a degree on the 67 talents of mankind. This will measure your talents and rank it from one to 67. It will help you to be aware of what your low talents are, but also to leverage your high talents to be even more successful than you already are.

Those assessments are available on my website at www.drhank.biz and if you'd like to get these assessments done for yourself, your family or your organization, contact me there.

I have used this incredible information throughout Corporate America with Chase, IBM, and in all the areas of real estate: company services, mortgages, real estate agents, and title companies. It is extremely beneficial.

It is insightful and helps you to get grounded to understand who you are. Some people say, "Oh, you don't have to be that way." We really don't have a choice.

I was at a dinner party the other night. One person, (a high influencer) sat at the head of the table and talked probably 98% of the time. This was for a 3 1/2-hour meal.

When anyone else said something, it was like this person couldn't wait to start talking again. You can see that influencers are driven to talk.

It bothered my wife and other people around there. It didn't bother me at all. I was simply observing. (You know the Bible even talks about being an observer, and I observed all these people and realized who they were.)

An influencer will love to talk, nothing changes that. If you want to be happy, one of the lessons here is to allow people to be who they are. When you do, you feel the heavy weight lift off of your shoulders, and you'll stand taller. When I allow them to be who they are, I can also allow myself to be who I am. Do this and you will find an immediate recognition, you will begin to see the positive aspects of people.

As that person at the head of the dinner table was talking, I could have shut down my shade. But, I kept it opened and every once in a while, he had brilliant points that were interesting. I was able to pick out about three good points that I would have missed otherwise.

One of the points he brought up, was that the middle class is growing in the next 20 years from a billion to three billion people. The middle class is growing which means that big corporations like P&G and Coca Cola are going to continue to thrive internationally.

My takeaway from this is that the world is getting better. There are big indicators on how everything is getting better. It's getting better for you too because you're being exposed to these positive thoughts that help you recognize the magnificent and brilliant creator that you are.

Beliefs Success Unit

Right now, I want you to answer two questions:
What beliefs no longer serve me?
What beliefs do I want to have that serve me?

If you think you're a sinner and that you're paying an awesome debt, maybe that belief is one to give up, because it sure doesn't feel good to me when I think like that.

When I think, "Wow, I'm made in the image of the likeness of God." I believe that makes me feel good, and that's what I want. I'm not here to pay off any debtor or try to prove myself to get to some other place. I'm here to create.

I'm here to sift through this and all beyond this world, all the perfect contrasts of the unwanted and wanted. It's all here and by your asking, Source can make more of it—more money, happiness, better relationships, people, and clients. It's all up to you to start asking for what you want and not giving a hoot about how to do it.

Our beliefs are how we have been told that we're supposed to do things. The world coming together, going upstream. I'm telling you none of our desires are upstream, they are all downstream. This is a whole new way of believing; for each one of us to start looking at the beliefs that make us feel good, and which beliefs no longer serve us—then leave those behind.

The amazing thing is that so many beliefs survive that are old and outdated. They really don't belong to us, they are inherited. The good news is; we can actually choose new beliefs.

You know I'm an ordained minister. And I share this with Christians, too. If you were born in India, then you wouldn't be a Christian no matter how much you fight that. There is not necessarily a right way or right religion. If there is a "right religion," it is as easy as this: You're being guided (not by religion and what they are saying and their opinions), but you've been guided by your emotions all the time, and that's your communication system with your Source.

Your bad emotions say, "You're not thinking about this as your Source, you're not on your path and the Source wants to put you on the path." The more pain there is, the more love there is because Source says, "Really, you're getting lost. You're one of my lost sheep, come back."

If you start thinking positively and start feeling better, then you start feeling that you're lined up on a call directly with God. You don't have to read it in the Ancient Book, but it's fine if you do, if it's helpful and makes you feel good.

But, know that most of our beliefs are not our own. We were brought up adopting these beliefs through mannerisms.

I was in front of my daughter-in-law at Christmas and was playing on the ground with the dog. My daughter-in-law, Michelle says, "Oh my God, you act like Chase," who is my oldest son.

She continues, "This is amazing. You have the same mannerisms!"

She was right. However, it was really Chase who was acting like me. We're looking at everything through our thought process, the way that we do things, the way of our mannerisms. We all pick that up, and we're like magnets. We are magnets that called that up, and we think that's how it should be. So we build beliefs in alignment with that.

As you focus more on the beliefs that serve you and the magnificent creator you are, your magnificent thoughts begin to create and the Universe revolves around you. As you think about those worthy thoughts, you ask your Source to come in, provide all, and believe that in asking, you shall receive. Be specific on how you ask, so that you improve your beliefs.

Prioritize Life Success Unit

This is prioritizing your life. That gets into time management and starts looking at what I call high-payoff activities. Most of us invest about 1/3 of our time in high-payoff activities, whether for our personal life or professional life, and 2/3 of our time in low-payoff activities.

One of the reasons why I can guarantee specific, measurable results and at least the 400% return on your investment with *Top Producers* is because I'm going to take those individuals who go through the process, and we're going to focus more on our high-payoff activities.

Imagine. If you can take your high-payoff activities from 1/3 of the time to 2/3 of the time, what do you think is going to happen to your business? What do you think is going to happen to your life?

On average, you'll start saving three weeks per year, and you'll be more productive because you're going to be more focused on your high-payoff activities. You'll be listing what your high-payoff activities are. Then track during the day what your low-payoff activities are. Most people don't even realize because they're used to going through the same daily routine. They don't realize how many low-payoff activities are preventing them from achieving all that they want. So it's an amazing session.

Emotional Intelligence Success Unit

We end on your emotional intelligence, which was accredited in the 90s and goes beyond what anybody knows of creative intelligence. Most of us, if you're reading this book, have a high enough IQ, (intelligence quotient), but do you have a high enough EQ, (emotional quotient)? More people are let go from companies because of their EQ than IQ.

As you care more about how you feel, the divine guidance system that runs through your veins will embrace your whole essence of who you are and what it is you care most about and recognize that you want to feel good. You will be guided into all that you want whether it's building your empire, your health, or relationships.

Create your dreams as you increase your emotional intelligence by paying more attention. To focus and ask for your dominant intent is to feel good. When you feel good, God leads you to the people, to the circumstances, to the events, thoughts, and sensations that will create your good feelings and manifest all of your dreams coming true.

CHAPTER 18

Becoming the Happiest Man in the World

I have shared experiences that have taken me to this place where I am joyful.

Something I have come to understand is that there are two great misunderstandings that have occurred for most of mankind that create much unhappiness and disease and cause much mourning. I want to talk about those two subjects today to enlighten and awaken us all to these misunderstandings. First, about death.

Death

Death is really a misunderstanding that prevents us from having our joyous life. Much pain is in the belief that there is death. It is done unto us as we believe, and if you believe that your loved ones have transitioned into the nonphysical and are gone, then they shall be gone.

For if you believe, it is done unto you.

Too much unnecessary grief has poisoned our lives. There is no greater misunderstanding and distorted various responses than to that which we call death.

We have been told that we have eternal life.

Yet, a loved one transitions into the nonphysical, and we think they are gone. Nothing can be further from the truth.

I would like you to think right now about your grandmother or grandfather who is no longer in this physical form. Can't you feel their presence here with you?

The fact is, they are right here with you when you call them in. All you need to do is ask, and they shall be with you.

Those who have walked before us, are eternally at one with each of us and interested in us—relatives, ancestors, even Christ.

Most people in the United States are Christians whose ancestors came from Europe; these are the beliefs that were transposed onto us.

We have been told we have everlasting life. Yet, when someone transitions, we think they are dead and gone. We do all this grieving.

If you look and feel the energy of those who are no longer in this physical form, you can feel these positive, beautiful feelings. To access this eternal love and infinite intelligence, we no longer need to look for where they were.

Most of us are looking for that physical appearance of those who have been before. There is much grieving and sadness that they are gone. For some of us, it is the rest of our life that we are in this place of not feeling good.

We all have a communication system within us that tells us whether we are thinking as God is thinking based on our feelings. It must be the truth when you are thinking that your loved ones are missing.

This is an abundant world we live in. It is big enough to hold all the interests, beliefs, and desires that you have. Everyone leaves this physical plane, and everyone we love rests within our heart forever more. What a comforting thought to know that is true and to know the power that we have. We, in fact, can ask for more and we will get more.

Think about this as God thinks about this. We must look where they are now, not where they were in this physical form. All those who walked before us reside in our thoughts and feelings, and are present now.

Death is really a time to rejoice, to look at all those who have transitioned from the physical to the nonphysical, because that is the only thing that has really happened here. Let us rejoice that there is no one missing. Nothing is missing in our life unless we believe they are missing. The abundance and freedom each of us desires is there for us for the asking.

We are called human beings. We are in essence beings in this physical state in this world. We are this physical being, but a much greater part of each of us is the nonphysical. We are an extension of this nonphysical energy.

When we transition, what really happens is that we are birthed back into eternity. It is my hope that you, your family, and loved ones may be comforted by these thoughts and know of our everlasting life.

This is the time to celebrate life, our own life and those who have lived before us, and to celebrate that our loved ones are alive and well. We can keep them in our heart and consciousness for all of eternity.

A Father's Letter to His Sons

My mother was close to transitioning. She had dementia and was lying in a hospital bed. I wrote a letter to my three sons who were in their 20s at the time.

I wanted to share a different perspective.

Here I was in the midst of, what some call, losing my mother. When in fact, I gained more of my mother, and a deeper, more meaningful relationship with her.

> *Hello Sons,*
>
> *I want to share my thoughts around our relationship, and how long we will be together. First, there is no loss in death.*
>
> *Death is only an illusion or better stated, "a misunderstanding." A better phrase for death, is simply a transition from the physical to the nonphysical. Even now, we are more nonphysical than we are physical though our attention is primarily on the physical.*
>
> *When I transition, I will only lose my five physical senses with my much larger sixth sense being well intact. This sixth sense is the feeling, an emotional state that is eternal and all powerful. It is this energy sense that far outshines the five physical senses.*
>
> *Your grandmother, Shirleen, my mother, is not using her five physical senses. Yet, I have a better relationship with my mother than ever before, because I can feel her presence with me. I have discovered the depth and breadth of Shirleen in a new and satisfying way.*
>
> *The sixth sense is far more accurate at defining and satisfying than the five senses we experience here on earth. We have focused ourselves more on our five senses in this physical form though this sixth sense is far more meaningful and endearing.*
>
> *All those dearly departed are with us at all times, and you will recognize this if you will simply focus on them. An example would be to focus on grandpapa, and he will be with you, or focus on Jesus Christ, and he will be right there with you.*
>
> *Something else that can provide you more comfort and relief is to call upon your spiritual family and angels. They are here for you*

to give you love, support, guidance, and help you gather your desires. You need only ask for their help and they will instantly be with you.

Due to my deep and endearing love for each of you, and your love for me, together we stand in a rich tapestry of an eternal relationship. Eternity is a long time, so know that I will be with you always.

Love, Dad

When my mother transitioned, I started to tune-in to my mother and her essence. When we transition, our resistant selves (our resistant personality) disintegrates. We are in a pure state of allowing. The prejudices that my mother might have had—for instance, when she thought I was the best looking son, or she would nitpick about my shoes, or the style of my hair—all of those resistant parts of her transitioned. I now can have the pure essence and love of my mother with me. When you allow that, you will be guided into amazing experiences in life.

Specifically, my mother used to do yoga. When her friends were in their late 50s, they stopped playing tennis, but my mother played tennis till she was in her 70s because of her yoga.

I had never done yoga. I think I did a couple of positions, and I said I'm not doing this. I was inspired to go to a yoga class after she transitioned. I knew this was my mother guiding me, in her loving, supportive, and pure allowing essence of who she was.

I went ahead and was guided. I asked for better health, to look more youthful, and that was my answer. It's not God or some mysterious thing. There are the people who have walked before us who are guiding us, too. In this case my mother was guiding me to better health and guided me to this yoga class. I didn't know anything. I was in this class, in my late 50s surrounded by young women 28 to 32 years old. Not a bad thing at all!

I had an amazing experience. When I first began the yoga session, I closed my eyes and took a deep breath. I started feeling my mother in all the cells of my body. I could feel her love. I could feel her presence there. I began to do yoga, and now I can do all the positions. I can even out-do some of the younger people in the class. I love it, and it is an amazing time to this day. I'm 62 years old, I do yoga twice a week (with my mother.)

Beliefs and Previous Life Experience

Let's go back to the beliefs with which you have been brought up since you were a child. When my grandfather transitioned, it was all kept quiet. It is like the topic of sex that we keep ignoring, too. People don't talk about it, especially with young children.

I was a child when my grandfather was suddenly gone and there was no explanation. They didn't let me go to the funeral. They felt because I was a child I couldn't handle that.

All of us have experienced thousands of lifetimes on this plane, in this beautiful world, this perfect contrast. We are not this little baby that runs the household. As parents, we have these resistant thoughts to protect; there is nothing to protect. There is no bad unless we call it forth into our experience. We were brought up thinking, "I have to be protected." So my parents protected me and then didn't share with me the understanding.

If I had this understanding that I have now, it would have been a marvelous experience. I could have felt my grandfather's presence at that young age.

They said he was gone, so I figured he was gone, and he was not here anymore. I didn't realize that I could tap into him. Right now, I am tapping into my grandfather and my grandmother, because they were little love birds.

I remember when they were older, my mother told me, "It's so sweet that they are lying in bed together, holding hands."

My grandfather wrote a wonderful little note. He said, "These words are meaningless to me. What is meaningful to me is, my dear and everlasting love towards you, Ulga." And he signed it, Love, Charles.

That's why we think it's missing—we have the belief; we were brought up thinking that it was missing. It is my hope that those who read this and are exposed to this information will share this with their children.

When we are born into this experience, we don't have any memories of the past. We are born virgins. To know our previous experience would clutter up our new experience. We are separated from our previous knowledge so we can be virgins and live this life joyously.

Then we are brought up with these beliefs that it is missing. It boils down to, what is done unto you determines your beliefs. We have been brought up to accept beliefs that are not our own. We have been brought up with these beliefs that when someone transitions, they are missing. They are gone and are no longer with us. That is the time to grieve and a time to be sad. That for many people lasts a life time. It actually prevents them from being happy.

As my letter to my sons indicates, this sixth sense is the magic of it all. The essence that we think of as the five senses is good and accurate yet lacking. I'm looking out the window right now on the 15th floor, and it looks to me that the world is flat. We know that it isn't. When I was out on my porch this morning, it looked to me like the sun was rising, when really the earth was turning and the sun is in the middle of it, and we are the ones that are turning.

Our senses are misleading and don't tell the actual picture. The accuracy of the sixth sense is impeccable. It is the means of all the senses to understand the truth, and it's the communication system with our Source.

Sixth Sense and Committees

Napoleon Hill wrote *Think and Grow Rich* in the 1930s, and it is the number one motivational top selling book of all time. Because his book became public domain, I co-authored with him *Think, Feel and Grow Rich*. I found out that when the book was originally published, they had edited out the word "vibration" 37 times. His book was considered so far out there at the time, that they said, "Enough is enough. We can't start bringing in this vibration stuff that we don't know," but he did write it. He had a whole chapter dedicated to the sixth sense.

In our book *Think, Feel and Grow Rich*, we talk about the sixth sense. It includes parts of his original transcript and my writing.

Napoleon Hill discussed having council meetings. It is the most fascinating concept. He describes how he would call on his cabinet members for the knowledge that he wished to acquire. He would call on:

Mr. Ralph Waldo Emerson to gain marvelous understandings of nature.
Mr. Luther Burbank to enable him to harmonize.
Napoléon Bonaparte to learn to inspire men and to raise them to greater lengths.
Mr. Charles Darwin to understand his patience and study of cause and effect.
Mr. Abe Lincoln and others, too.

None of these people were in this physical form in the world. Napoleon Hill had these council meetings in his imagination where he desired to build into his character a keen sense of justice and untiring spirit of patience. He also called in:

Mr. Dale Carnegie, who in the early 1900s, was the wealthiest man in the world.
Mr. Henry Ford, when he asked for the most helpful of people who could supply him much material essential to his work.
And Mr. Thomas Edison.

One of the great examples on how real this was for him was how he developed their individual characteristics because he studied them. For example, Lincoln had the habit of always being late to the meeting, then walking around in a solemn parade. You could see him walking slowly with his hands clasped behind him. Once in a while, he would stop as he passed, and rest his hands upon his shoulders.

Can you feel the presence of that council meeting? Each of us can have our own council meeting.

I'm going to share with you what I call committee meetings. I have a couple of different committees I'm playing with. My kind of stable committee, the members on that committee are:

Jesus Christ
Martin Luther King
President John F. Kennedy
Abraham Lincoln (He rests his hands on my shoulders and paces back and forth.)

I'm asking for these desires, this wisdom, knowledge, and understanding. It's comforting to know that we each have all the intelligence that is and that has walked before us. We have this infinite intelligence to ask and receive this amazing knowledge. They literally will give and send us energy because we are all vibrational energy beings.

So are those who have walked before us, and we can call them forth. If I have a computer issue, I call Steve Jobs in.

Now, when I call Steve in, he first says to me, "You know, Hankers," we always laugh when I call him in. He says, "Hankers, I'm really not the technology guy, I got other people doing technology. I'll go ahead and help you with your little computer problem you have. You can't get 'Word' working, right?"

That is an easy peasy piece of cake for him.

My wife, Sharon will say, "I have a computer problem."

Now me, in my physical sense, I am not a high tech guy at all, but she says, "Can you please, bring in Steve to help me?"

I sit down, and I'll be guided. I touch a couple of tabs and all of a sudden it is working.

It is amazing how you can call them in and who you can call in. Each one of us has this power, this ability to call in, they are right here.

Not only are they right here, they have this amazingly, deep and meaningful interest in you, a love for you, and they want to support and guide you to all of your desires.

The beauty is, because they stand in this pure state of allowing as pure Source energy, they know where we are. They also know where we want to go, and they know the path of the most allowing.

So you can form your own committee in the same way that Napoleon Hill and I have. I have this one committee that I have relied on for years to guide and help me. This committee helped me recover from a broken neck when my C1 and C2 were hitting the stem of my brain. I was told I would be in chronic pain the rest of my life, which I wasn't going to play a part in, so I started to create this committee. They came in to help me.

Before a speaking engagement, I call them in. They are the greatest speakers that have ever lived, and I call them to help me perfect my words and body language, and my tone of voice. Most of us are so concerned with the words that we use. It's not our words at all. Our body language makes up 60% of our communication to someone. Most of us are not paying attention to our body language. The tone of our voice makes up 30% of how we communicate. And, only 10% of communication is with the words that we use.

We get things backwards, and think that we get the outside world by manipulating the outside world. We will never manipulate the outside world by starting from the outside. Everything starts from the inside.

Start with *The Joy Shop* to create the way you want it to be.

My Angels

Now I'm going to share with you a more recent committee of seven. One is an infinite intelligence; this being is amazing. One way to look at this and to call upon in a gentler way, is to believe and to know that you have angels. It's a nice way of saying, I believe in angels. The Bible speaks about angels. I like that idea of angels. Well, this committee is made up of angels; my seven angels.

Infinite Intelligence

The first Angel is one of Infinite Intelligence. This supreme being knows how to awaken my self-consciousness and my divine self. That is the first one I call on that comes into the committee.

Vision and Unity

The second I call on to develop my vision and to unify the world. What I do is call in the committee, and I'll ask, "I want to build these deep and meaningful loving relationships that sparkle with people who gather up and help me with my desires."

Wisdom

The third angel is to call forth wisdom to evolve the world and come up with new thoughts that have never been. This angel I ask to put thoughts out in a way to touch people's minds, to awaken themselves to their divinity. They think in their mind of who they are, and their divine heart recognizes who they are.

Intuition and Harmony

The fourth angel is to deepen my intuition and to harmonize. I want to first harmonize with myself, then to have harmony with the world and all that is.

As I ask to increase my intuition, I tap an even greater source, to gain clarity into these magnificent beings, to provide beautiful insight and be helpful to me to navigate in this physical form.

Freedom

The fifth angel is to achieve my liberation and experience more freedom. The *Number One* reason we are here on this planet is for growth. We are automatically going to grow. We are living in this beautiful world of contrast, that tells us what we don't want, that burst into new ideas, new feelings that have never been before.

The *Number Two* reason we are here is to experience more freedom, and to feel that freedom. Consider Martin Luther King, and how he had his dream. This dream is freedom, more abundance in our life.

Idealism

The sixth angel I call in is to embrace high ideals that I want to give to the world. To free ourselves, to have this new idea about the magnificent being, that each one of us is.

This is what this book is all about, high ideals to free ourselves from the chains that we use to lock in the beliefs we have wrapped around us, for instance, a belief that there is a death.

Divinity in Form

My seventh angel is to create divinity in form, and I love that. To take these divine ideas and to put them into form, to uplift, and inspire the world to have all of us experience more growth, more freedom, and the prize for joy.

Clarity

Joy is the prize. Realize that we can have joy right at this moment. Some of us don't have that clarity, and we're saying, "I'm confused. How do I get there? How do I get to that joy?"

One way to look at it is to realize that in this moment you can be guided to the next step on your lighted path. We may not be clear on a lot of the different things, even on what we want. But one thing that all of us can be clear on is we always will know how we want to feel.

All of us want to feel better. If we start there and say, "I want to feel better in that I would rather be happy than sad. I'd rather be rich than poor, fed than hungry, lifted than be deflated. I'd rather be powerful than weak, focused than confused."

I always know and how to be led to what I want by getting in that whole mode of feeling yes. I want to feel good, and because I know that, that will lead to clarity one step at a time.

You're not going to have all that laid out so you can see the next 20 years, because you don't want it all laid out. The next 20 years can be harmful to your personal experience at this moment. Now, that doesn't mean you can't listen.

When you're looking for clarity, start with this: "I want to feel good."

When you ask, then you receive. I guarantee you that it's gathering for you those thoughts, those sensations, people, circumstances and events that will make you feel good.

Feeling good is all any of us want.

Many times we have thought if I have enough money, I can be happy. When you think that you have to have certain things first before you can be happy, it's backwards. Know that you need to be happy now, and you'll have the money, you'll have the things that you want and the different desires that you have, the goals that you will become, do, and have, everything that you want by saying, "I want to feel good, show me the way," and you will be shown the way.

Divine Guidance Team

Each of us has a divine guidance team, and they are always there with us, we can always rely on them. That's why we're never alone. That's why there's nothing missing. The more we recognize them, the more connection we have with them.

When we recognize that we can call on our divine guidance team, our council members, our committee members, our angels, people who have walked before us—however you want to position that—they're all there with a deep interest.

The happening place in the whole Universe is right here and right now. His place will be always right here. Why? Because it expands all that is. You have had love for your grandchildren, for grandparents or your children. You will have a love that has never had emotions that has never been there before to that degree you currently have.

You're so important to the Universe because this is the place that's happening. We're creating it and making it happen as we go beyond where thought has been before, which is what this book is about.

Going beyond thoughts, some of the words I think have never come out of my mouth. They're in my mind, they are expanding all that is. It's taking every one of us right now together. There's nothing like this togetherness, that one plus one is equal to three. As we expand our thoughts we expand all the energy that is. As we expand not only thoughts to place us as its number but, but we also expand energy. We expand all that is to places that have never gone before, and that is what it's all about.

The beauty is that's exactly how life happens. We're in the spiritual form. We came into this physical form and then that took us to the plane where we wanted to be. In this physical form there are many delightful things that we want: different people, different thoughts, and different circumstances. We have everything we want and everything we don't want.

Death is the first misunderstanding, the one that creates unhappiness. That's why these two topics have been brought up, because it creates a lot of confusion, and a lot of unhappiness. I think we all now realize and said, "Oh my gosh, there is no death."

So, we say, "Hallelujah," to that.

Sex: The Second Great Misunderstanding

Just as we are blessed with a magnificent world in this physical form, we are blessed to have sex, the second greatest misunderstanding.

Sex has been equated to sin. If we consider how most of us were brought up to think of sex, your existence could be considered an act of sin. Most of us have been taught that sex is something you shouldn't do, that you should not enjoy it, that you have to be married in order to do that. Enjoyment of and partaking in sex has almost been raised to the level of being a personality fault. It's like, "Oh, you shouldn't go to such base physical senses."

If you want to talk about misunderstanding a word that word is sin. Isn't this what you've heard over and over: It is a sin to have sex. Sex is not good. It's a weakness of man. It's sex in Adam and Eve.

How about considering this perspective, instead: "Sin" was an archery term in Christ's time, which simply meant, "you're off target."

You're not thinking as God thinks if you believe sex is a sin.

With sex then, is it something to be embarrassed about? I was masturbating in my bedroom, when I was 13 years old, and my mother walked in. The first thing she said was, "Oh my God! Don't do that!"

Sex is also a topic not discussed in most families. My mother never said a word about that incident afterwards. Why not? It's like something that's shameful. There's where the word shame comes in. We feel shameful that we masturbate, or if we speak about sex to someone.

Well, the truth is, we're all having sex and pretending like we don't. There is this drive, and it's this internal deep desire, it's actually part of our soul. The Soul's desire is to experience sex. That statement probably has never been said before.

As we go in and start looking at this, it's one of our key desires as a physical, human being. What creates a strong desire for us to have sex, so strong that we'll have it alone if no partner is available?

It's powerful in a relationship, these deep feelings towards each other, and sex is great. But, it's something that most are uncomfortable with. In fact, most even seek to hide from it being in their experience. People pretend that it's not there. Parents pretend that it's not there, in front of their children it's, "Oh my God, what would the children think?"

What do you mean what would the children think? All the children grow up and have sex, too. That's how we have people.

For example, a woman wants a baby, and even though she's going through the physical action of sex, she still doesn't find herself with a baby. Sex is part of the physical process that facilitates the greater wanting. But, the greater wanting must also be aligned before conception can occur. You have the power of the mind over the body. If you're not in alignment, you can have the physical act of sex and not actually create a child, even though you want to. We know there's this deep desire.

What is this deep desire? In this case, sex is for the perpetuation of our species. It is inherent and is a deep seated desire. All of us have this deep seated desire to multiply.

The Angels Are Envious

Sex is about two things. One is to continue the species so that more beings can come and experience this amazing world and lead us to a much greater world. We come back in because we have desire, and as we create ourselves, a small part of our non-physical will turn physical. You pick your parents and you'll be conceived. I know most of you think you didn't have much time to pick your parents, but the fact is that you did.

The second reason for sex is for the purpose of enhancing your experience. We've been talking about the process of joy. Being without sex cannot be a joyful experience.

So many think birth control is an evil. Birth control is a decision to have sex without having a baby. That really is no evil. Rather, all things are a choice, and we have continual options to have the freedom to choose as we want; to have sex for a reason of creating more people, or to have sex to enhance our experience. The two most difficult conversations married couples have, are money and sex.

Males and females have a desire for sex. It is something that they don't talk about. Sex seems to cause many people problems, so much so that it is commonly attached to negative emotion. What's the problem? Oh, I have a negative emotion. From what? My upbringing.

Nobody talks to us about this. The only thing that I was told was pretty risqué at that time. I went to a class with my dad. It was a sex class. He was saying, so you put your penis into the vagina and you come out with a baby. He didn't talk about the great experience, the climax or the clitoris. I didn't know what a clitoris was for years. My poor girlfriends. Nobody talked about it. I didn't know. I thought it was the vagina. It is part of it.

Again, that word is seldom used. One time I recall my children where in the car, about 13 years old, when Eminem (who I would call M&Ms) came on the radio and he was rapping, "Yeah, on the clitoris." So, I asked my sons, "Do you know what the clitoris is?" No way, they had no idea what a clitoris was. Because of these beliefs, sex is typically shrouded in lack of talk, misunderstanding, and a lot of negative emotion.

What is negative emotion? It means I'm not thinking about this as God is thinking about this. So, sexuality has been so distorted; it brings about attention to lack. It brings attention to lack of what? Primarily lack of worthiness, to the lack of righteousness.

It's been called a "weakness of man." It puts us into a state of where we think of a lack in limitation. What is lack in limitation? Think about a circle cut in half. One half of that circle on any subject is the unwanted which is lack and limitation, and the other half of that subject is the wanted, abundance, and joy.

Most of us, because of others' beliefs, have been brought up to believe that sex is sinful. It's a bad thing. It's a weakness that you don't have to do it but, if you do it, it is kind of terrible. It's a mish-mash: part I want to do it and part I don't like this desire.

So we have this negative emotion that creates a lack of worthiness and righteousness. In reality, sex is an amazing aspect of our amazing human experience. See, we have the power to create our experience any way we want to. If you feel like, "Oh gee, I have to go and do that again (have sex with your wife or your husband)," then what type of experience do you think you're going to have?

You create your own experience. We are creators of our own experience, to include our own experience of sex that can be absolutely amazing or not. Sex is a coming together, to co-create another being or another experience. There are infinite ways to have experiences on this earthly plane, in this world. We have the choice whether we want to have a good experience or a bad experience.

A similar experience can come together in the minds of two people or the bodies of two people. This creates a greater sense of joy and freedom and growth if we allow it to be. We are all seeking harmony, and a truly satisfying sexual experience is when two come together, the purpose of that harmony, for the purpose of each, of our being uplifted by the physical expression. It's amazing.

I'm telling you, it's like the angels are a little envious of this one. Boy, they can't wait to get back down here. They want to have one of the greatest physical expressions you can have—sex.

Be Happy and Together

Any time two people come together for any experience whether it's sex or something else, it is more satisfying than being by oneself because we are all up lifters. It is wonderful to be happy. Absolutely. Don't we love to be around happy people?

When you're happy, you're a magnet to attract all kinds of happy people to you. You attract what you are. What you are on the inside determines what you are to the outside world. What you are inside attracts to you whether you attract ordinary people or happy people.

Clarity, who do you want? You know you have clarity. I want to be a happy person, and I want to attract happy people. Do we not find our joy even more magnified when we are having fun with one another?

Sexuality is two physical beings coming together in a physical way to experience more than one experiences singularly. The reason there is a climatic point, the point of ecstasy, is because one coming together with one in harmony is amplified. One plus one equals more than two.

But many of us say, "Oh yes, I remember that, exquisitely delicious and exactly in the way that it is intended. I had that a few times and no longer."

That is due to one's attention to lack. It's like you think you are robbing a gas station or something. Or the two of you are normally in that harmony together but something feels strange.

When two people are in harmony together and have great sex, it is like icing on top of the cake.

When two that are out of harmony in every other way and expect to find harmony in sex, it should come as no surprise when they can't find harmony in sexuality either. This can turn sex into more of a mental thing than a physical thing.

When you have the pleasure of coming together in harmony with one whom you are in tune with emotionally and physically then, you'll find the ecstasy.

It is your belief that affects your experience, and your distorted beliefs about sex creates an unwanted experience. As you relax your old beliefs, and think about what you want, then you shall have a better experience.

All you need to do is to believe that there is sex here in this world for two reasons: procreation and for the experience. Having sex to enhance your experience will be everything you dream it to be, when you give up the shame, guilt, and the attention to lack.

In *Think and Grow Rich*, there was a chapter in the original book that talked about sex. Transmutation, as Napoleon Hill puts it, is the mutation, in simple language, the changing, or transferring of one element or a form of energy into another.

The emotion of sex brings into being a state of mind. Sex transmutation is simple and easily explained, which means switching of the mind from thoughts of physical expression to thoughts of some other nature. Sexual desire is the most powerful of human desires.

It's your soul's desire to have sex. Why? To procreate, to create more beings. What's the prize? Joy. One of the ways is physical. We are physical bodies, and we experience physical connection together that we call sex, in a way even the angels can't do.

The first step is don't try to figure it out because if you try to figure it out you try to manipulate right there. I mean this is a horrific word, and nobody wants to be manipulated again, because it takes away our freedom. So, don't try to figure out the past. This is about everything that you are not enjoying as much as you know you could.

What you do is start looking specifically to sex. You look at what you want to have your husband or wife be. Ask to seek to have them be your soul partner, your best friend, and the best lover in the world. When you put those together, and you start asking, Source will start creating the next step for you.

Don't Look Back

I have clients who want to lie on my therapy couch so they can talk about all this bad crap that has happened in their life. And I won't do it. I don't give empathy because it creates more of what they don't want.

We can go forever digging up crap. We can dig up all this crap, but it won't get you to where you want to go. We are so conditioned to dig up all the trash from before. When I focus my attention, it grows and gets bigger, so that trash will become more trash full to the brim and my cup will overflow of crap. That's what I don't want.

So don't look back because your experience is misleading you. They were different circumstances. There's a different energy.

The new you who is going through this whole thought process together with us is different. You are at a higher point of attraction, a higher level of energy. You are becoming awakened and enlightened, which means you can do all those things you did before so long as you're inspired to do that.

They'll work this time. They didn't work the time before, because you were attracting the low vibration which you didn't want, and that's why it didn't work.

So point one, don't dig up the old trash. You're not going to figure out what happened.

Then point two, stop trying to figure out the "how." How do I do it? What do I need to do? If you are trying to figure out how, you are focused on the problem and not the solution, and you won't fix it.

When you have trust in God, full trust, and you give your full self, your body, mind and soul, you say, "I relinquish that control. I give it to you to take me from my desires."

You are not this puppet being led by the Source, you are saying, "Here is what I want, take me to it, I give up. You do it."

Look for Positive Aspects

Your next thought might be, "Wow I'm going to only look for what it is that I ask for from the Source." This one is a big one. Look for positive aspects in yourself and in everyone else.

Let's take for example, this thought: my spouse and I don't have good sex. How do I move from there?

You only think, notice, and talk about positive aspects of your sexual relationship. Maybe he is a great kisser, maybe she is really cuddly, you get the picture.

Focus on what is working! Focus on positive aspects.

I'll give you an example, my wife, Sharon, said to me, "You know your gut is getting a little big." Now, I'm thinking for 62 years old, I'm in my best health. I'm slim, trim, and fit. She thinks I have a little gut.

I shared with her if she would look at positive aspects, she could let go of paying attention to that, and it would help me to trim down. If she continues to pay attention to my stomach, it will only help me have a bigger stomach. Whatever you focus attention on grows, in this case a bigger stomach.

In that example, I could start by saying, "Hey Sharon, look at my strong arm, the good curve on my chest, my strong legs and my muscles." I could shift her focus to some positive aspect.

When you start looking for positive aspects in your spouse, you will start seeing more and more good, and you'll start seeing them change. You will both start growing. It is one step at a time.

Here's another thing, when you are focused on wrinkles, guess what? You're attracting more wrinkles or signs of aging. Stop looking at the wrinkles. You could have anything instantly done.

Normally, we have to do it one step at a time. Know that everything is getting better in your life. If you believe that, and start looking for that, it's possible.

To have more money and more abundance in your life is to seek and then find what's positive that's playing out for you financially.

If you look at what's playing out for you, you're automatically telling the Universe, "Give me more of it!" and soon your life will be filled with so much abundance of money, time, harmonious people, great sex, rendezvousing with your relatives that have transitioned, with having these committees to having these spiritual guides, it's system and people, that their beings there that are tapping in to all that is, it will get better and better for you!

You can have it all.

For the person who says it can't get any worse than this, it can and it usually does.

Why? Because the whole attention and focus is on "getting worse."

And you say how does that happen?

Well, there's everything that you want. There's no judgment. Whatever you're thinking about, you'll be getting more of it.

Think about what is playing out for you, and I'll guarantee you, you're going to have all that you want. It may come in a little bit different form that you may have thought of, it won't necessarily be a pay raise, but it could be an inheritance or a lottery.

There are an infinite number of ways to create more abundance. All you need to do is to allow it in.

CHAPTER 19

Health and Youthfulness

One of the things we sometimes ask for is health and youthfulness. Then when it doesn't go the way we expect, we expand on some contrast we have like a pain in our elbow. When we feel that twinge, then we go, "Oh this is awful. I ask for good health and look what happened? I've got a pain in my elbow." We start making a big deal out of the little pain in our elbow and that leads to the law of attraction which leads to creating more pains and more discomforts and diseases.

That gets us right back to where we were, and puts us on the other train, the train that goes on upstream, being difficult, and being a challenge leading to being unhealthy, and getting older and looking aged.

For example, right now look at your body and how much it is doing for you; your digestive system, your ability to think and to read, to see and hear, to breathe, and your circulatory system and heart to pump nourishing blood throughout. There are so many good things playing out for you, providing the health that you do have. There is so much good going on with us, but when we brought up this little contrast of a painful elbow, we think it's the end of the world. I encourage all of us to look at those little pains in our elbow and say, "Hey that's what I don't want."

Even more so look at all the things that are playing out for you, because there are amazing things, there are a thousand fingers weaving from your thought, creating the type of life that you want. And you want those fingers to weave good health and youthfulness.

There is No Such Thing as Dying

We transition from this life to the next life. But, even more important and more appropriate for this subject is that our bodies are literally regenerating themselves 24 hours a day, seven days a week, 365 days a year. Our liver regenerates a new liver every three months. A year from now, 99% of your body will be a new body with new cells. Focus on the 99%! Focus on your ability to make your new cells even better than your old cells!

So, we use our calling forth for good health. Literally, every one of the atoms and nuclei within your body are being transformed for what you're calling them to be. That's why people can overcome a bad heart or a bad stomach or whatever they want because of the power of our mind; we literally regenerate better than before because we think to ourselves (think to Source), "Oh, this is the body I have for the rest of my life."

The fact is you have literally billions of cells dying and new ones being birthed every moment transforming your entire body. That's why when you call forth, "I want to be healthier, and I want to be more youthful," you can, because your body understands that energy. You're calling forth with your thought energy and that energy then is interpreted into better health, better functioning organs, better functioning body, better circulation, better digestive system, better sexual system, better senses.

Begin to think and feel, "My eyes are getting better, I'm hearing better, I'm seeing better, I'm smelling better." Get yourself into this beautiful, physical world. You have an amazing energy behind your thoughts to be birthed into this world, and you have this great, great desire to be in this physical world. So, enjoy this physical world, enjoy your senses, enjoy your ability, and then do it with your Source.

If you can't smell so well right now, ask your Source to smell it for you and through you. Smell with your Source and you will start smelling better because your Source smells it perfectly. So smell perfectly!

Taste with your Source and get into your taste buds and have them start becoming robust.

Have your ears and your eardrums responding perfectly and start hearing the sound of the Universe coming to you. When you do, you'll start hearing things like the birds chirping. You'll start hearing the symphony voice, the tone of voice from people. You'll start to appreciate and you'll start to see the beautiful world out there, a world that is filled with love and with joy and with more freedom for you.

The more things that you want, the more the world offers you. When you were making the choice to come here, you didn't come here to pay off debts. You didn't come here to prove yourself. You didn't come here to get to some place that's called Heaven. Heaven or Hell is right here on earth. And we've created our entire experience we are having right now with our thoughts.

So rather than wallow in our pity party, thinking about how tough it is and what's not working, and crying over spilled milk, why not start saying, "I'm going to start calling forth the way that I want my life to be. I want to have a healthy life. I want to be healthy. I want to look more youthful."

I promise you, as long as you stay on that without being disturbed by what's going on in front of you, by what your senses are telling you (remember they're not telling you the truth of what the reality is) and not being impacted by your circumstances that you currently have, because all those circumstances are whether it's some health issues or looking older or whatever, it's merely the accumulation of your thoughts that you had previously. So you can stop and reverse that.

Literally, you can reverse the aging process.

You have the power (as long as you believe it), to reverse the aging process and to call forth your health and your youthfulness, and when you do, it will come running to you. Whether you realize it or not, you transform your body in every moment. Your body cells are living, dying, being created, regenerating. You are born again. That's why every morning you wake up, and you're born again. You have the ability to focus on what you want in your future, and not think about what happened in the past, what happened yesterday, the bad stuff, and what's happening right now. Again, you don't want those things. They are unwanted. Stay focused on the things you do want. Then it will be possible to get those things.

CHAPTER 20

World of Plenty

Let's say that we've landed in the world of plenty, and there's plenty of everything to include plenty of time; a world in which we're given an extra 24 hours in a day.

It's all fun and wonderful. This chapter is about relationships and we're going to have a powerful understanding now about how to have relationships play for us and someone else. I have information to understand why we even have relationships and how to have these relationships to do divine will and to live a life of our divine self and the life of our soul.

Relationships offer us a means to expand.

We're here for three overall reasons. If you want to know what your soul wants and how to live a life in harmony with your soul? Then, it starts with these three general areas.

I want more freedom.
I want more joy.
I want more expansion.

With relationships, you expand with others to help us reach our dreams.

If fact, if you didn't have other people, you couldn't be who you are because it gives us this opportunity to grow and expand. Every person that you interact with is a part of the person you are becoming. Everyone contributes to our becoming, so it is to bless all people. For many, that is difficult. We think, I can bless everybody except for my ex, your parents, my old boss or whomever.

To see how everyone has been a blessing to you, you should take and receive relationships as your Source receives and understands them to be. Other people help you find your preferences of what you want and what you don't want. Even unpleasing relationships have value as they help you to define what you don't want. It's impossible to know what you want without understanding what you don't want. Other people have shown you through the years, things that you want as well as what you don't want.

What you want to do is pick the things that you do want from different people and to embrace those positive qualities. An example: a person who's wealthy, but has a lousy relationship. They seem to be unhappy. We can't assume money causes unhappy relationships. You can look at that person and use them to help you define your preferences. You can say, "Okay, what I don't want is to be unhappy, so what do I want? I want to be happy. I definitely don't want to have a bad marriage so what do I want? I want to have deep, meaningful relationships." Take it a step further and you will probably see many benefits to being wealthy. You can ask for that, too.

Meaningful Relationships and Communication Shades

Creating meaningful relationships comes from a soul level. It's an amazing journey. We'll start first at face value.

I've mentioned that Hippocrates in 330 BC recognized four primary behavioral styles. At that time, everybody was farmer. It wasn't about relationships, and people were more interested in basic survival. In the last couple hundred years, many, many things have occurred allowing most people to have a better life than before.

Warren Buffett has talked about babies being born into the world now. He said, "They're the luckiest group that will ever be. Even though the politicians are saying the world is going to hell. The world is actually getting better. Look back 200 years ago, to where the world was, compared to where we are now. We have running water, electricity, automobiles, computers and whole libraries, and our food. Overall everything is getting better. We all want to focus and turn our cheek to the things that are getting better."

We look at people's behaviors one way: we open up the curtain of communication that most of us have been taught to keep closed and guarded.

We have this shade, and if people's behaviors aren't like ours, we have the subconscious tendency to pull down our shade and shut them out.

God looks at all of us as angelic because we're divine. We're made in the image and likeness of God. So, if you're thinking differently about someone in a negative way, you know that you're not thinking about this as God is.

I don't even want you to care anymore about what other people think of you. Instead, I want you to care most about what you think about other people.

When you are understanding what you go through here, you'll start caring about other people, and you'll see positive aspects of other people. You'll start to experience more freedom, because those who are tied to being people pleasers restrict their own freedom. Their disability is caring more about how you feel about other people versus how others feel about you.

The more that we understand ourselves and the more that we understand others, the more we can raise that shade of communication with ourselves to ourselves as well as to others.

We are all of these behaviors. Normally, we're real strong in one behavior style, pretty strong in another, and the two other behavior styles we're not strong in at all.

We need all the behaviors and all the different types of behaviors to make the world go round, to give us that contrast, to give us the means to expand, and to improve our preferences through other people and other people's experiences.

A great way to retain and embrace this information is to think about people, what category they might be in and allow them to be who they are. Theirs are God-given behaviors—as are yours.

D.I.S.C. Personality Profiles

Here, briefly, are the four personality types based on DISC.

Driver or Dominance

It's easy to remember that the "D" is for the driver or dominant. These people typically like to do a lot and are focused on the bottom line and accomplishing results.

See the big picture
Can be blunt
Accepts challenges
Get straight to the point

They like to control and they like to demand. They are happy to be demanders, and they go to this and go to that.

They are good at making quick decisions, but that doesn't mean they are good decision makers. These people are often considered dominating and can be seen derogatorily, especially women who are drivers. (But the fact is, we have been taught through the ages, not to judge. This whole chapter is going to help us to no longer judge other people.)

So, the D, the driver, is typically rough, tough, makes quick decisions, hard, firm, and fussy.

The way we want to be with the driver is to be efficient. You want to answer their questions right away, get to the point. They don't like long drawn out stories.

For example, if they ask you, "How are you doing?" Answer quickly.

If you start a long drawn out story by saying, "Oh, I woke up this morning at 5:00 and I had a great time doing *The Joy Shop...*"

You know they don't want to hear all that.

They want to hear, "My morning was fine. Let's move on to the purpose of the meeting."

That's the driver. About 80% of the population are drivers.

Influence

We use the "I" for influence. The influencers are out-going, and they do a lot of talking. They are known for openness and relationships.

Show enthusiasm
Are optimistic
Like to collaborate
Dislike being ignored

The best way to be with the influencer, is to be stimulating. Speaking to an influencer, rather than say, "Hi Sue. How are you doing?" in a flat tone, instead, I kick it up a little and go higher and faster in my cadence, "Hey Sue, how are you?"

I'm talking about 100 words per minute, the influencer's mind is going 300 words per minute. It keeps their attention.

Steadiness

We come now to "S" for steadiness. The steadiness person is, "Don't rock the boat." They don't like change, and they are about cooperation and being dependable. They like to keep things normal.

Calm manner
Don't like to be rushed
Supportive actions
Humility

They are all about keeping an even pace. You have about 40% of the population who are steadies. I always say the reason is that the D's and the I's, are so outgoing that they would rock the boat over. With 40% of the population with the S, we don't have the boat rocking over. The way to be with them is to be agreeable.

So what does "be agreeable" mean? It means don't say, "No." They will automatically shut their curtain on you. The word "but" will do the same thing. If you say, "Oh, that's a great idea, but..." The "but" word erased the statement before, so they hear "that's not a great idea." People don't feel good with that. It's like, "You're not hearing what I'm saying." Instead, what do you do to be agreeable? Change "but" for "and." Say this, "Oh, that's a great idea, and have you considered..." It's a completely different answer! One that Steadiness people will appreciate and listen to.

So again, you want to identify these behavior styles (typically within seconds) so you can better communicate and relate to others. Modify your behavior style a little. Recognize who they are. What you do is open up that shade of communication so you can more effectively communicate in their language.

Conscientiousness

We then move into the "C" for conscientiousness. These people are about data and facts. They like quality, expertise and competency. Some might stereotype them as a fuddy duddy accountant sitting in a corner.
Enjoys independence
Objective reasoning
Wants the details
Fears being wrong
Only 14% of the population is primarily C. These people like a lot of data and facts. They are all about rules and regulations. The high C's say that rules and regulations are to be followed. Medium C's say rules are guidelines, and the lower C's say rules are made to be broken. We have to watch those low C's!

Give them information about whatever you're offering or explaining to them, and your perspective on it. They want to have as much information as possible. Make sure the information you give is accurate!

Peeling Back the Layers of Personality

This is face value, when looking at people's behaviors, and how to build ideal relationships. That's really what this whole chapter is about—how I build ideal relationships and have some answers. This is one way, when you're in front of someone, or if you're talking to them, even if it's through email, you can start understanding their different behaviors. It's like peeling back the layers of an onion. As we peel the onion layer off and go a bit deeper into people, we see that each person has their own language based on what they value and what motivates them.

We have all varying degrees of values. One of the values that you want to have is to speak people's language. Language is knowledge. Those people who want knowledge are in the highest of all decision making motivations.

In contrast, other people will make decisions based on what I call utilitarian or a return on investment. Those people are more interested in having the language speak to them, to provide all the knowledge.

If you'd like, let's take a look at this with the Six Motivators mentioned in Chapter 16.

Think about that Utilitarian/Driver. People value that you shared a lot of knowledge with them, but they wanted to know the return on investment; only the necessary information. If you don't do a satisfactory job of that, you weren't speaking their language, and they will shut down their curtain.

When people are high in one area, and typically most of us are real high in one of these values, we don't understand why other people don't value it. We speak our language about what our values are.

By understanding these other values, it will help you to understand that people value different things. By understanding their discussions, interests, and the questions that they have, you'll discover their different values.

That summarizes the behaviors to begin with the face value of behavior. Then you go into what people really are valuing and how they are motivated.

Honor and Praise Others

Each of us is here to help each other expand and define our attributes. This contributes to the expansion of us as eternal beings. It is an amazing world that can accommodate the full variety of all the interests, beliefs and desires that we have, and realize that this world holds the space for everyone's desires; all the desires that we have and more. Sometimes, we only think in lack.

An example would be, I have money, therefore I'm taking away the money from somebody else. That isn't the truth on how life works. When I ask for money, Source makes more for others, too, whether it's money or whatever. This world holds all of the interests, beliefs, and desires that we want. Which means, there's no one out there, based on their desires, who would limit you having your desires. When you are open and allow people to have their desires and to be happy, when your heart can sing for the happiness of other people and the abundance of other people, then you're in a place that you will allow for more abundance for you and everyone else.

Others provide the variety for us to choose our behaviors, our emotional values, responses, personalities, characteristics, our attitudes, moods, and our reactions to the situation. None of this variety jumps into our life.

What does that mean? The people who come into your experience are those you attract based on your emotions. If you wake up honoring that, I can guarantee you that you're going to run into honoring people. Every piece can be alpha to the omega. They can be really good and wanted by you, or they can be unwanted. It depends on how you're thinking.

The choices that others make have nothing to do with your experience unless you allow them to. Everything comes to us through our own vibrational invitation. We are the inviters that are sending an invitation to attract the type of people who we want to have an experience with. Not only to attract the type of people who we want, but to attract the people who we already know, to attract the positive attributes that we want to see from those people.

We have been told that old people can't change, and that you can't change other people. Everything comes to our vibrational invitation, and they will remain only by our continued invitation until we change our thoughts.

We Are the Creators

We live in a world of freedom. Everyone has the freedom to choose what they give their attention to. Thus, what you choose to experience are interactions with others. This provides us the contrast that assures continual expansion. The Master of the Universe, God, is more in your relationship. This creates more expansion of your emotions than have ever gone there before.

Those of you who have children, think of your children and your love for your children. Those are emotions that were never there before. The thoughts of your love toward your children expand all that is. It does not matter what another's choices are, what their desires are. This is in no way to deprive us of our desires.

That is why there is no competition in this world, even though you've been brought up that there's competition. There is no competition in this world and there is no one preventing you from having anything that you want. Why? Because of abundance. There is nothing to compete for. We each can have what we want. You are the creators of your life. Know that to be true.

If you are inspired in this life experience to have something, it's certain that this desire will be fulfilled. This world will have the potential to deliver us all of your dreams come true. There is nothing that is preventing you from having anything that you want. You are the powerful creator who can attract anything into your life.

We can all bask in the value of differing opinions, and this allows us to reap the harvest from every relationship. Those relationships that you thought were bad, those were simply relationships that showed you what you didn't want so you could birth the ideas you do want, and that will lead you to better relationships in the future.

We cannot think or feel for another. You will find great relief as you allow others to be who they are and allow yourself to be who you are, even as you feel opposed to others in their perspective. This interaction provides you with a basis for expansion and solutions and answers.

Make peace first with yourself, then with others, and accept them for who they are. Seek the benefit of their contrasting opinions as this gives birth to an improved situation and a better life for you.

Imagine every relationship is set up for you in order for you to have a better life. As you focus that attention on what you want and who you want, you will start attracting those people you want into your life experience.

No one has the power to negatively affect your experience unless you allow them to. It is only your response to others that has the power to pinch you off from the good feeling person that each of us is naturally.

Being reliant on the behaviors and opinions of others to keep you feeling good will never withstand the test of time. Others are as changeable as the wind and can cause you to change your behaviors or your opinions as easily.

The only reason we desire anything is we're made to feel good in having it. The only way to feel good is to be aligned with your Source, and with these expanded solutions and answers that are being held steady by your Source, by your God.

Who Really Changes?

Are you a people pleaser? Does that get in the way of you feeling freedom, joy, and being present? So then, you may say, "Okay, I'm not going to be a people pleaser anymore. I realized that it's all upstream. If I try to please people, I'm not going to get anywhere because they're going to continually change in their preferences and thus, I'll never really please them."

What can you do to take the current relationships that you have that are somewhat challenging and make them better?

The one key attribute to change, which most of us have been trained the opposite, is to look for positive aspects in others. Start looking for what you want in others.

> *I'll give you an example, I have a lady who has been married for years. She said, "You know my husband is the worst. He doesn't trust me. He doesn't trust me with money. He doesn't trust me around other people. He always keeps an eye on me. And, he doesn't compliment me."*
>
> *She went on and on. (Sound familiar?)*
>
> *I was not empathetic towards her. I would not put energy into this diatribe. She eventually recognized my reticence and said, "You know you're not getting into this like I am."*
>
> *I said, "No way, I would never want to embrace and start creating with you more of what you don't want. What you're telling me here is all about what you don't want. Now tell me, what do you want?"*

She had to stop and think for a second. Most of us probably have to think, especially in those challenging relationships. What would I like to see in those people?

Here's another misunderstanding that we have been told, we can't change anyone. The fact is she was attracting that, so after I asked, "What do you want?" She said, "Well, I want him to trust me and support me, to compliment me, to be kind to me, to be supportive of my job."

She started building that energy. Within a couple of weeks, she came back and said, "Wow, my husband's been changed."

But who really changed? It was her that changed in her thinking. Why? Because we're the creators of our experience.

My great example that I use is my father-in-law. His name is Sledge, like a sledgehammer. It's a threatening name. When I first met him, I drove with Sharon to visit her family and she told me all about how bad he is, and how he's never been kind to her boyfriends. He wasn't kind. She shared this with me.

I started saying to myself I'm going to be positive. I've never met the man. What positive aspects do I want to see in him? I thought, I want him to be kind to me. I want him to be talkative to me. I want him to show me around. I want him to be nice to me. I want to have a great time with him. I want to enjoy myself with him, and he with me. I want to have really good conversations with him. So, I started this energy. I started to pre-pave my relationship with him before I even met him!

We're all full of energy. We're in the center of the Universe. For us to call the energy of our preference to us is remarkable. Let's say, you're going to a holiday meal with the relatives. And, you don't want to see your cousins because they always talk about you. The more that you hope they don't say "this thing" about you, the more they're going to say "that thing" about you. You're attracting it into your experience.

The Universe only knows about vibration.

It doesn't know if you've said "do" or "don't." It's the same signal to the Universe. Know that by thinking, "I hope they don't say bad things about me," you're in that moment attracting them saying bad things about you.

Instead, when you focus on the positive aspects of others and pre-pave the relationship you want to have with them, you'll start seeing that more and more of those positive aspects will appear, and the aspects that you don't like will leave you. Think about what you want to see in others, and you will start seeing that in others.

We Choose Everybody

There's not one person you know who you didn't attract to your experience. You even attracted your parents. I know some of you don't believe this or think you didn't have enough time to choose or didn't do a good job of it. The fact is that you choose everybody into your experience. Understand that among those people in your experience, you can choose the alpha to the wanted or the omega to the unwanted based on how you're thinking about them.

Start doing this now and change the attributes of people you are in relationships with now if there is something that can be improved. Look for the positive aspects and the good in other people, and you'll start seeing them change. Know it's a wonderful thing. Not sure you can do that with some people? Start doing it with someone you can do it with. Or, like on new people!

You have the power to change those key relationships into harmonious ones. I call forth harmonious people into my life. I love harmonious people. You can start expanding that and say, "I now call forth into my experience harmonious people, fun, worthy, bright, happy people."

Start getting into what you want and start asking for it. If you think you're in a world where you walk outside not knowing what you're going to get so you wait for a surprise, that's not how this works. The way it plays, the way life is, when you walk outside, you're going to start attracting those people who you're thinking about overall and people who you want to attract. If by chance, you have an exception where you attract somebody that doesn't meet fit the bill, all that means is that your previous thoughts generated that. Don't pay attention to it, pay attention to how many of the great people you have attracted, harmonious people, loving, kind, understanding, funny, and witty. As you do, you'll get more and more of those people. If you focus on the exception, the exception will become the rule. You'll end up with disharmonious people and people of the unwanted. So, to that end, we no longer have to be a people pleaser.

We Are People Pleasers

We, for the most part, are brought up to please others, our parents, teachers, our friends. You have been brought up to be a people pleaser.

There are times where you notice someone is happy because of your behaviors and that makes you happy. But no one's happiness can depend on how you behave. If others come to rely on your behaviors for them to feel good, then both of you will end up unhappy for you can't keep up with pleasing yourself and understanding what pleases others.

We came here with the anticipation that we would experience more growth, and others would significantly contribute from our contrasting differences. Others provide us more choices, but contrast the unwanted on the physical plane then birth an equivalent of the wanted things in the non-physical dimension. As a problem is taking form in our experience and consciousness, there is an equivalent solution that is taking form at the same time. This new and improved non-physical vibration is then held steady by our Source.

All we need to do is be this vibration of the answer, of the solution and we will manifest it into our experience. This is eternal joyous expansion at its finest. This is why we are each so important and essential to the Universe, to God, as our role of joyous, free expansion contributes to all that is, in the most significant of ways. This is so powerful to embrace, to realize that when any of us experience a problem with the relationship in any type of situation, at the same time the solution and the answer are being birthed for you. As long as you let go of that problem, the relationship, and the issue that you're having, and instead ask for the solution that has already been birthed, because it's being held steady by your Source waiting for you to come and meet Him. Once you meet that vibration of the solution, there'll be an answer and you will then experience it in your life.

Before we came here, we knew that every problem has a solution. Every question would bring us an answer. It is for us now to ask for that answer instead of talking about that bad relationship, putting it on Facebook, or texting others about it. Ask for the answer instead of sitting up in the middle of the night, rolling around about how bad that person is or how bad that situation is. You won't find a solution there. So, instead of doing that, give all that up. That's going to birth this amazing solution, to be the type of future that I want, the type of blissful joy that I deserve, expect, and believe to be mine.

We, each have the ability to focus on the direction of solutions and answers with no aversion to problems. They are part of the process of eternal expansion. We are the ones relishing in the joyful aspiration and exploration. First, focus on what we want. This is co-creation at its finest.

What is the Most Important Relationship?

Many of us believe the relationship with our spouse or with our children is the most important relationship, but good luck with that! I know someone who right now is losing her children because they're growing up, and they're finding their wings.

They are flying to their freedom, their life, their experience, and to their joy.

This mother is so used to playing that role and thought that is her most important relationship. But as they each release that relationship as being the most important, and instead point to Source as their most important relationship, they will discover their most important relationship is not with others at all. It's between you and your Source, your inner being.

If you make this relationship a priority, all other relationships shall be grand. They shall all fall into place because you're flying high when you're rendezvousing and dancing with your Source.

All the other things that you want, the people, circumstances, and situations that you want will come to you because you're an attractor of what you want.

When you're sitting at that place where you are at one with your Source, one with God, that you are in a place of feeling good, of joy, of being happy, then you can have anything else you want to offer another.

We're thinking about the things we don't want, and we're unhappy. That vibration that we're unhappy goes to the people we love, to our children, our spouse, whoever.

What does that do? That puts people down to that vibration rather than expanding them to their highest being. We must realize that we have Godly, Divine things to offer others. When we are divine, we are aligned with our Source.

If you think and behave based on what keeps others happy, you will lose connection with your Source.

As you align daily doing the things we discuss in this book, doing *The Joy Shop*, your consistent happiness will be the example to others. It is the power of your example that shows the way to discover the same freedom and joy for themselves.

We are connected. We have a chord that connects in this together. A chord of common love, common Source, common growth. We have that. To lift up yourself and the world, the most important relationship is you and your Source.

Give up the impossible task of pleasing others. Stop caring about what they say. This shall set you free and take you on your lighted path.

Go to the path of least resistance by showing others your alignment and thus your happiness. When you are aligned with your broader perspective, aligned with your Source, caring more about how you feel than anything else, then your focus shall uplift others, and divine relationships shall come to you.

Your gaze upon others will then be tuned-in to seeing success for others. This is the greatest thing to give others. It's your all-powerful thought for their wellbeing.

Not what they're going to do if I'm not still there.

What are they going to do if they don't have whatever we've been giving them and enabling them with?

Instead cut them free and that will then cut us free to realize that we are all free to create as we so choose.

Go to the path of the least resistance. When you are aligned with your broader perspective and aligned with your Source, caring more about how you feel than anything, then your focus will uplift and the entire world will gaze upon others.

It will then be turned into seeing success. Your attention to their success and well-being harmonizes with the point of view of your Source. It becomes that as you are focused on your relationship with Source, it will help them to focus on their relationship with Source, creating the happiness and the good feelings that we all desire.

You will align with your success and your wellbeing, then you can offer the infinite resources of the Universe that are now available to you, and that can shine on others.

Chapter 21

Divine Relationships

When you start having a relationship with your inner being, your soul, your Source, it is a way to understand how to live a divine life and to live your soul's life. Those words are nice, but how do you do that? I wanted to share how to go to the nonphysical, to your Source, to divinity, and start creating now.

The ideal of a divine relationship is in the eyes of your soul. Your soul has a purpose and intention for you down here, in three areas: more growth, freedom, and joy. For us to let go of the ideas of relationships and what ideas we think, how this role should be and whether it's in the significant other, marriage role, children/parent role, or whatever.

Start letting go of those ideas, those pictures in your mind, the expectations that you have, these are all from your analytical mind and they all came from the world. They weren't yours. You were brought up with them and now you can let them go. Then feel your harmony in yourself, in everyone and everything in your life, a way to know, to start connecting and start having a divine mind, and heart.

Start Connecting

To really start living the path and will of your soul is to begin to connect your loving heart with your wise mind. We each have (no matter how many scars) a beautiful loving heart. Most of us have chains around it so that no one can enter. Let go and unlock those chains. Open up your loving heart and wise mind center.

Imagine there is a connection of this beautiful divine light that connects your heart, mind, and the center of your soul. By asking, call your soul in and ask your soul to rest in the center of your soul's essence. Feel your soul all around you, loving you, connecting you.

You are now strong together with light connected with this divine light. Feel your soul's light all around you. Feel the love and the radiance from your soul that begins to open up your mind and your heart. Allow this connection and this radiance from your soul. Hearing the call from your soul, you're now transferring this love and life. Take that love and life that you now have. You are all connected as one: the soul, the mind, and the heart.

Extend the Connection

Start extending that out to others. Think of the relationships you want to transform into divine relationships. Ask to experience new consciousness.

I'm going to go through seven areas here as you are at one:

Ask to experience a new consciousness.

Ask for a new realization of your relationships.

Ask to initiate the true activity of your soul and the divine relationship that is possible between that one person or all the people who you know now and will know in the future.

Ask to link your personality and your old beliefs with this divine understanding. As you call forth this new consciousness, each one of us is powerful. We simply have to ask for this new consciousness of divine relationships and allow it.

Ask to unify these relationships and establish loving relationships.

Ask to use your magnetic quality to draw the ideal relationships. We are each like a magnet. You have the magnetic quality that you want to ask to draw these ideal divine relationships into your experience.

Ask for the gift of clear vision in the eyes of love.

Look at love in all these as I had with my father-in-law, Sledge. Sledge had his arm around me showing me this stuff in his office. He was smiling, he was talking to me, he was love. I'm looking at him, and I want to share with him, I love you.

My wife, Sharon, was in disbelief. She had never seen this from her father before.

You can transform any relationship into this beautiful defined relationship. All you have to do is ask for the gift of clear vision in the eyes of love. Ask to evolve, bring about, and receive divine will. Let go of all your current understandings and surrender the need for any more effort, work, and need to please. Start asking to evolve these relationships into divine relationships.

Ask for beauty and harmony and release all limitations.

Imagine yourself in the middle of your quiet place within your soul where all possibility surrounds and encircles you. Release any limitation and feel any limitlessness of you. Turn any conflict into harmony, call forth a higher energy of expansion balance in harmony. As you call in that energy, this is an energy world, a vibrational world.

With your thoughts, you have the ability to call forth all of this beautiful, loving, positive energy of the Universe into your experience and create into every one of your relationships. Now link your higher mind with your analytical mind to connect your thoughts with divine thoughts of your relationships.

Think of the divine image being angelic and running around with the other angels. You are all angels. All these beautiful souls running, playing together, having fun, and enjoying what we came here for, to enjoy, ask and simply receive.

We have given up all the struggles, the work, the pleasing, and realized these magnificent creators. If we can create it, we can call forth the energy. There is an unlimited amount of energy to call forth by all of us to have anything and everything that we want, to include these divine relationships.

We will now be given the thoughts and inspired action that bring about a transformation that happens easily and automatically as you ask to connect with your divine mind and the divine mind of others. The key here is not only for you to be connected to divine mind, but that you want to connect yourself to the divine mind of each of those souls in the relationships of people you know and those who are coming to you.

Ask for causation to harmonize with the souls that you know. Let go of your lower mind and expectation and ideals, and instead embrace your soul's ideals. Know that all you need to do is to say, "I'm going to let go and allow my soul's ideals to come to me."

They will come on every breath to you. They will become more evident in your life. Your life will become more divine with more divine relationships.

Let go of your motivations to be saved, to be liked, and to embrace everything that shall cause your ideal relationships to be realized. Simply ask to express and produce order, harmony, and love with everyone in your life.

Call forth and receive these energies and you will bring about these ideal relationships, and it shall be done unto you. Bring energy of light to your soul to express the beautiful relationships and perfect harmony that you call forth between yourself and with others. Allow these energies to pour into you and be surrounded by the radiance of these energies of your soul and all the love that abounds. Let it be placed in your heart center. Imagine and feel the light and the love going out from your heart center to the person or people who you know.

Take one person that you know and take that loving energy from your heart. Pass it to their heart. You will see magical relationships starting to abound in your life with all people no matter what the past has been. You have the power to create any and everything in your life, including these soulful relationships. This love is flowing out to your people and creating ideal relationships. Simply ask for divine will to manifest all your relationships and create the ideal relationship with all people now and forever more. So it shall be done.

There are many people who can embrace that and there are many more people coming. We are literally holding the doors open for people to walk through these doors into the corridor of joy with deeper, meaningful, and divine relationships.

CHAPTER 22

Healthfulness and Youthfulness

We have the power to create good health for ourselves and we'll share it in this book. There have been many who have walked before us who have created good health when they didn't have good health.

What I am talking about here is really how we think about what most people would call aging. The word aging infers certain things that we've been exposed to since we're born into this world where we have seen mass consciousness in action. The effects of aging are a reflection of mass consciousness and false beliefs about aging. So even though this chapter is about aging, this chapter is really about youthfulness and about our health.

You have witnessed others having old age and aging. You have perhaps witnessed the same in yourself. You have experienced the type of thoughts that come up when we use the word aging versus youthfulness.

Aging takes all of us to many areas of lack, of limitation, of powerlessness. I would like to help you, and all of us, start bringing these old thoughts into the light of illumination from our divine self and to literally disintegrate these past thoughts, beliefs, and experiences that you have had since the moment you were born into this world.

As I've spoken about before, contrast is a beautiful thing. This is what this world is about, everything we don't want and everything we do want. I'm going to share a lot right now about contrast, about things we don't want.

Think about your health and where you are. I'll guarantee you're going to improve that health by reading this chapter, by listening to this, by experiencing this and awakening and understanding.

What we don't want is contrast.

Health, Aging, and Mass Consciousness

First of all, this word aging which is all around us that we're exposed to. Think about what it typically means and what people think about it. They think about less energy for example, so to achieve the opposite of less energy I call forth more energy into my life.

We think about things like aging as wrinkles and whatever we focus our attention on, we get more of. If you're focusing on the new wrinkles you have by your eye, you'll start getting more wrinkles because we are the creator of our experience. Instead look for the smooth skin on you, on your face and wherever you can find them. Focus on what you do want, not on what we've been so used to. The lack of perfect health in the world is the perfect example that we have really been caught up in mass consciousness.

Thought comes to us from two different ways. It comes to us through the world which I call mass consciousness, or it comes through the divine mind. When your thoughts about aging come to you primarily through the mass consciousness, this is going to bring up less energy and wrinkles. When your thoughts come from the divine mind and are focused on perfect health, you have more energy of life and smooth, soft skin.

Another result of getting your thoughts about aging from the mass consciousness implies that aging has to be about getting older. It doesn't imply that I'm getting better, rather it implies, for example, trouble walking.

Think about you might have said to yourself, gee when I'm in the walker someday, that's creating that. It's one moment after the next but the law of attraction and all that is God is going to come rally round whatever our thoughts are. If you think at some point in our future that you are going to be in the walker, in the wheelchair, well it's pretty much guaranteed that is exactly where you will be.

Think, for instance, about aging and your grandparents.

I saw a TV commercial about a Buick. There were two young women talking, and they said, "Oh that's a Buick. My grandfather or my grandmother is probably driving that," insinuating that anybody who drives a Buick is old. Then out of the car pops this young, handsome man. Now the two young girls say, "Wow."

You see, their attitude is that when you're called grandma or grandpa, then you're old and you're not hip. It's these subtle insinuations that happen to us, we start believing this is what happens with aging. Whereas think about a grandparent you know that they told you, "Oh, I'm going to be a grandparent" and you're thinking that young person is going to be a grandparent. This is the opposite of what we normally think a grandparent to be: old and grey and walking slow.

Thoughts about aging, for example, include arthritis, frequent urination, lack of erection, and pain. These thoughts thrive because they're making more money. Think of how many commercials you've seen that focus on all of these things that are associated with being old.

Think about TV programming. Commercials like these program us for what we don't want. The more we see them, the more likely we will be to have what the commercials show.

The mass consciousness is filled with thoughts that tell us that pain is one of the biggest things associated with aging. Everything you read, hear and see says that as we get older, we're going to have pain; our joints are not going to be good; and the list goes on and on. You can put yourself in an old person's body fairly quickly as you think about this concept of aging. Don't do it. When you come to pain, think instead, "I want to feel good. My joints are lubricated and feeling good."

There's always the opposite because in every subject, one side is the lack of and the other is the abundance of. Let's look at the abundance of your health and even flow into youthfulness, because that is not associated with aging and not being focused on frequent urination.

> *As you know, I broke my neck, and I healed myself. Yesterday, I was at lunch with a man who read my bio. He said, "Oh my gosh, my wife broke her neck and her C1, C2, and C3."*
>
> *I said, "Oh my God, I broke my C1, C2 and the stem on my brain was hitting the little broken parts."*
>
> *He said, "Yeah, so the doctor said, 'Oh, it might be cancer.' Oh, my God!" (And, we're honoring the god of other people's opinion especially when it comes to health here.) We start thinking oh, we might have cancer.*
>
> *In this case, the doctor told his wife, "We're going to go ahead, and we're going to purge those C1 and C2 and C3." Well, then he is telling me that about a year and a half later she had to go in again. They had to purge the C4. They did the C5 in another year and a half. Then six weeks ago they did the C6. This all*

started about five years ago. Now, they are going all the way down her back, and continuing to cut off the flow of wellbeing.

The fact is there are instances where we need doctors, medication, or an operation. The fact is also that we do have the power to heal ourselves.

Here I am in perfect health and feeling youthful. Whereas this lady with the same condition that I had, continues to have one operation after the next. How many times have you heard about people who are getting a knee operation or a back operation? Those are other big ones.

I have a friend who has had five operations on his back. Doctors can't figure it out; we have it figured it out right now.

The answer is that we have wellbeing flowing to us and for us to put faith in that. Too quickly we jump into the world and the mass consciousness thinking that we need to have them fix us when we are not broken.

If you do have pain, try not to pay attention to it. If you have faith in God and in your Source, you will feel only wellbeing within yourself and you will heal yourself. That is powerful news for us. We have the ability to have good health and even to create youthfulness.

We don't realize this as a child hearing comments like "your grandparents are getting old" and "they can't think well anymore." They make up names for this loss of memory like dementia. They prescribe pills, creating what we think are the solutions for aging.

Ask for Good Health

We have these embedded beliefs from the time we are children that when you get old, you get wrinkles, you lose your memory, and you don't walk as well. Think of one part of your body. Let's start with your face. Think about what aging implies with that word "face."

Look at your eyes. Oh yeah, they get worse. About seven years ago I went into the eye doctor because I wear glasses. They said my eyes were getting worse. I said to myself I'm not going to buy into that. What I'm going to buy into is that my eyes are going to get better. Two years later, I went in and they checked me and my eyes were slightly better. They told me they would get worse, they haven't. They've gotten better. See how powerful we are?

We have the power. If you want to do something really magnificent, try this if you can't see well. Look at something like a little code on the back of a bottle and ask your Source to see it for you. Allow this to happen, and you will use the eyes of your Source and see the small lettering. The reason we don't do this is most of us don't believe.

Why don't we believe? Because it has never happened to us and we did not see it happen for the people who walked before us. Thus we don't have an example of it. You don't think or even consider that your eyes are getting better, much less having your Source see perfectly anything that you want it to see. You don't ask. Ask and you shall receive.

You have bought into this idea that aging means continuing to have these negative effects, but negative effects are things we simply don't want.

Think about your ears. What thoughts come in your mind with aging and your ears? "Oh, I don't hear as well." This is a myth, but you know all kinds of people who have lost their hearing as they age. The ear doctors say your ears are getting worse, and you start believing it. When you believe it, it's done unto you as you believe. As you start believing it, you get worse hearing. I've been conscientious about saying that I have great hearing. I know people who have hearing aids, and they are trying to make them real small so nobody can see.

All of us need to be conscious of what we say to ourselves. We don't have to have bad hearing because of age. We don't have to have bad sight because of age. We can start calling forth what we want as far as our health and even our youthfulness, to become good looking and feeling younger.

How about smelling? Oh yeah, I don't smell as well as before. Think about your teeth. I haven't had a cavity in how many years? They say that they are going to get old. You are going to need dentures. I don't buy into that. Every day I say to myself, I am so glad my roots are so entrenched into my mouth. I love my teeth being so strong. I start talking and making this stuff up in my mind. I convince myself, then I start seeing it in my experience. In this case I have strong and healthy teeth.

I had a dentist tell me three years ago, "I think your bottom teeth will probably fall out in a couple of years."

I'm thinking that's not going to happen, and I'm not going to do that, but you have these people who they have seen that it's true.

They say, "Look at so and so's experience..."

Anybody else's experience is simply their beliefs. These beliefs are getting passed down from generation to generation on aging. We have seen a change where not everybody has bought into this mass consciousness.

We start seeing Mick Jagger is still singing, and he is in his 70s. So many of these people are still singing; your voice and throat don't have to go bad.

I remember Tom Jones (Who I actually met once backstage in Las Vegas when I was with Jennifer.) Tom Jones was a friend of Anne Otis. Back then they were saying, the way he uses his throat, he isn't going to handle it, and he will only sing for a few more years. I saw him in the last couple of months on a TV show, still singing. People like Tom Jones are starting to realize, "Hey,

I really can create my own experience." It's time for each of us to realize that we can do that as well.

A few other things as far as areas of our body is our neck. Let's say, you have pain in your neck. The pain in your neck comes from pain in your thoughts. That is the only place that pain in the neck comes from. Thoughts that you don't want that's where you get the pain.

That is where all of this disease comes from because every one of these symptoms of "aging" aren't symptoms of aging. People talk about how your organs and heart might be clogged up with cholesterol and everything. People buy into this. Start seeing your heart healthy and your blood flowing freely.

You can clear out your heart by stating, "I'm going to clear out my heart. My veins are clear, and my heart is strong. I love to open up my heart. I am going to open up my heart fully because there is nothing to guard."

There is nothing to defend. There is nothing to protect. I am the creator of my experience and the only thing I have to protect is my own thoughts and then create into my experience things that I want.

You can do this with every part of your body: your arms, your hands, your legs, your ankles, your feet, and your sexual organs. Affirm what you want. Affirm that you are feeling better and growing younger!

> *One of my clients has a 92-year-old mother. She finally agreed to move out of her huge mansion and move into a care center. For $5,000 a month, the care center would take care of her. As they were moving her stuff, she wouldn't help at all. She was out with her boyfriend. She had a boyfriend for the last year and a half and they were always out together. The movers packed her things up, and they found her KY Jelly.*
>
> *They go, "Oh, my gosh, what is she doing with KY Jelly?"*

The daughter who is 65 years old says, "Oh my gosh, KY Jelly?"

The movers in the other room hear that, and they break out laughing. They can't believe it! The daughter goes to her gynecologist and says. "I want to tell you about my mom. We found KY Jelly in her room."

The gynecologist says, "Oh your mom needs type of lotion to put in there so she doesn't break her skin." Then the gynecologist also said, "I have scream cream to give her, for more lubrication."

The daughter is beside herself. These people are 92 years old, getting it on, and loving it.

Then, mom needed outpatient surgery. The daughter took her there and brought her back to her home so she could recuperate.

Daughter says, "Listen, Mom, tonight you need to stay in."

Mom says, "No, no, no. I want to go out with my boyfriend."

The daughter says, "No, you can't. You have to stay in."

The mom was upstairs resting, and the daughter went upstairs to check on her. As she got up the stairs she could hear her mom say, "Oh gosh, it's my daughter. I've got to get off the phone."

Here she is talking to her boyfriend, and the daughter says it is like the roles have changed.

I said, "Yeah we don't need any of these roles. Your mother is as happy as can be, but you think for whatever reason she needs to be a patient up in your bedroom. That she should not be having sex. Your mother is living the life of her dreams. It is you that is spoiling your day by having resistant thoughts about what you don't want for your mother."

You look at the ankle, feet, all these parts of the body where we have these perceptions. We think that our sexual organs won't work after 60, or whatever age we make up in our minds. When in fact we have 90-year-olds younger than we are.

Studies show that men in their 90s are the happiest guys in the world. There are few men living currently in this physical form so they have their choice and their pickings of all the women. They bounce from room to room depending on the night or day. The fact is that it doesn't have to be that the women live longer.

Be Open to the Divine Perfection

See? You look at what other people's experiences have been, and we say that is going to be true for me. You don't have to make that true for you anymore.

There is light and your Source (God) energy is this light energy. Light goes out from our divine self when we ask for this light. Ask for light to go from your divine self to these low-level thoughts, to these thoughts of people's experiences and to disintegrate them. You can actually turn it around and say you are getting more youthful. (I have meditations that can help.)

Release these thoughts and fill yourself with the divine light with the perfect body. Allow yourself to be open to your divine perfection.

How many times have we heard, "I'm only human. I'm not perfect." That is another belief that prevents us from being the magnificent creators that we are and to have the power to control our experience the way we want it. We have all been told that we are not perfect; we use this as a crutch to keep us small.

Instead, believe that everything is working out perfectly right now. In fact, your Source is happy and delighted with you. You are at the perfect spot, the perfect place that you expected to be in this lifetime. Everything has played out perfectly.

What a gift for you to be reading this information to enlighten and awaken you to even greater health now. The perfection of who you are is real; you are made in the image and likeness of God. Nothing is more perfect than that. This is not blasphemy or bragging.

I promise you that God smiles down on you that there is the light in you. That is perfection, and you are perfection as you are going through this world.

Going through this contrast identifies the things that you don't want such as poor health, aging, and getting older so you can focus on the things that you do want: good health and the perfection of your body, the light of the divine flowing to and through you.

Creating this life energy is perfect. If we focus on what we want and how we want it to be, then we will each start experiencing better health and more youthfulness.

Recognize the Power of the Divine Self

We need to recognize the power of our divine self, that we are only a small extension of our Source that has come into this physical form. That extension is perfect and when it is aligned with your Source, you can have health and youthfulness. This is the life God expected you to have and that you expected to have; to have a healthy, long, happy, and prosperous life.

At the time when you want to leave this physical experience, then that is the time that you do. In essence, we all commit suicide because we are the creators of our own experience. We determine when we're going to do it. We don't allow cancer to determine or whatever disease that is coming our way.

We start recognizing the power of our divine selves. Most thoughts we have experienced are not for our higher good. Think of all of these things that I have shared with you on this one subject, health. How many negative thoughts are there not for our higher good?

Now that we are illuminated by our divine self, we can start realizing each day on every breath, better health, more youthfulness, more vitality, more of the things that we want. What we are doing now is changing our future and what we want to draw to us.

What we have been doing before now is subconscious. We have created by default. We have allowed whatever to come into our experience, but today in this moment we are changing our future and the good health and youthfulness that we want to draw to us.

See our perfection of our divine self, of our healthy and youthful self. Release the other thought forms and create new divine thought forms for yourself. New mind thought forms are only thought forms that we have accepted and allowed in that we call beliefs. We have the power to change these beliefs. As you see the perfection of your divine plan of health and youthfulness, think of the image that there is a divine plan for each one of us. The divine plan is not one of getting old and having all these symptoms that we talked about. All these things that we don't want, all this missed health if you will.

There is a divine plan for each of us to have good health and to have youthfulness. Our good health and youthfulness is illumined in the thought of God. The thought of God about you is your good health and youthfulness. All you have to do is to ask for these new thoughts. These new illuminated lighted thought and insights.

There are so many things on this subject that affect this—the food you consume, the medication you take, the supplements that you ingest. Think of those ideas when you think, "If I eat this chocolate cake, guess what is going to happen to me? I'm going to gain weight and get fat." That doesn't have to be true. We have the power to literally transfer any type of food into our molecules and cells saying that they are healthy for us. When we do that, they will be healthy.

This Food is Healthy and Tasty

There was an experiment done with children who were fed a smorgasbord. It was available to them all the time. It included everything. There were vegetables, meats, and there were desserts. Initially the kids ran and got the chocolate cake ate that, got the vanilla cake and ate that. As time went on, they started being guided by their own inner desire. They started eating a balanced meal, including more vegetables!

A balanced meal is what is good for us, and we are guided to the things that will sustain our bodies and improve our health and will help us with our youthfulness.

We literally create our experience down to the cells of the food that we eat. Whatever food you have, bless that food and say, "This food is healthy and will nourish me. It will be good for me to be younger and healthier and feel better." Then it will.

We have the power to change anything. The three steps to all of creation are based on all the sciences, quantum physics, and molecular biology. All of them have agreed that the first step to creation is our thought. Thought turns into the energy that we turn into matter. We can turn any piece of food into healthy food.

When I was growing up, we were told that we are supposed to have dairy as one of our food groups. (Remember, I grew up in Wisconsin.) Now, nutritionists are saying that isn't true. Who is right? These people from 30 years ago? Or the nutritionists today?

You are right. You decide this is what is healthy for you. If you want to have supplements, then you can have those supplements. As you start working through that and listen to your inner guidance, thoughts and ideas will come to you. These will be for your health as long as you are thinking healthy.

Someone said to me the other day, "Wow you look great, how many pounds have you lost?"

I said, "I have no idea. I don't focus on my weight. What I focus on is my good health."

My weight has nothing to do with my good health. If you gain one more pound, who cares? We put a lot of stress on ourselves to eat right. What happens is I fall off the boat and go through the KFC drive thru, and I think that is bad? KFC chicken could be good for me, but because we've been told that it's bad by the scientists and the people who know, we freak out. They don't know squat.

Attract Ideas and Thoughts for Health and Youthfulness

Hundreds of years ago they were telling us that the world is flat. They were telling us that the sun goes around us. Humanity continues to evolve our knowledge and our understanding, but I am sharing with you we don't have to rely any science or anything in the outside world, including this mass consciousness, this worldly thought.

We can rely on our own divine guidance system to give us everything that we want. We are starting to dissolve these old beliefs and when we start asking for divine perfection, it will start radiating this good health and youthfulness to you and through you. You are going to have thoughts and ideas that come up in the next couple of days or weeks, and as long as you continue to flow with that, for the rest of your life.

Thoughts of good health and of youthfulness. Let's talk a bit about youthfulness. The fountain of youth people have been looking for forever? It's where everything else is. It's right within us. We create our youthfulness or not. We all want to be youthful. You are a fountain of youth, right here and now, when you say to yourself, "I now attract the ideas and the thoughts for more youthfulness. I love the idea of feeling and looking more youthful."

That's a great one if you could put that on your refrigerator, it would direct you to everything that you want. Who is directing you? God is directing you, your Source is directing you exactly to what is best for you for your youthfulness. If you say, "Yeah I'm getting older", that's what is going to happen. You change your language and you change your thinking process and you start talking about being youthful.

This is a powerful statement and there is nothing wrong with it, "I want to be more youthful feeling and more youthful looking. I want to look younger." Don't we all?

Change Your Momentum

Every morning I say to myself I want to look younger, and I giggle. It raises my point of attraction. I have people on a regular basis come to me and say that I look younger and ask what I did.

This is what I do, I ask for it. I ask to become more youthful. That is the power that we have to create our good health and use it. Again I refer to *The Joy Shop* because it's a great place to make these statements.

I control everything. I take no medications, no prescriptions at all. I've been recommended to take them, and I don't take them. I feel youthful, and I feel great. Let's say I experience a pain in my right knee. Rather than think about my right knee, I think about my left knee. My left knee feels great! Keep your focus on the things you like and the things that are playing out.

For each one of you, you have something that is within your body that is playing out for you, that is working perfectly. Your heart is working; you woke up this morning. There are so many things to start getting changing to build your momentum. This is all about the momentum that you create and because of mass consciousness we have this natural momentum of getting older, aging, dying, and misunderstanding all these negative symptoms.

The fact is you can now, right now, turn the other cheek and start looking at your good health and your youthfulness, and it will be yours.

Let me go back to health. A great example is someone who is in *Top Performers* right now. She's a large woman. When we're talking a little about health, she described herself as a full-bodied sexy lady. The way she said it, was like, "Wow!" She really is a full-bodied sexy lady. She is healthy and I love her attitude!

I'm 62 years young. That's a complete opposite of what most people say. You can see that using "old" with our age is a negative. So how young are you? If you have an interest in someone's age, ask, "How young are you?" You will see their eyes light up and get a completely different feel from asking them how old they are.

You want to be careful with your word choices.

I love saying that I'm 62 years young because most people don't think I'm that age. I want to be an inspiration to other people and realize that this age thing doesn't have any effect unless I allow it to. I'm proud to be 62 years young and I love that it makes me feel good!

The Three Step Recipe for Your Perfect Health

I will share with you my recipe for perfect health. It's three simple steps.

Step One: Feel good feeling thoughts

What does that mean? Start asking and start reaching. Imagine taking your right hand out and reaching up high for the next good feeling thought. You'll start getting good feeling thoughts. Right now in an instant, I could tell you a bunch of things that are not playing out the way that I want them; I don't pay any attention to them. I only focus on the good feeling thoughts that make me feel good because I know this will create the momentum to create my experience.

I'm becoming these good feeling thoughts, I'm doing these good feeling thoughts, and I'm having these good feeling thoughts about money or good health or whatever the subject is.

Disease isn't something that's contagious. Like cancer, it is disease. To eliminate disease is not going to chemotherapy. I've heard of many people being healed of cancer without having any chemotherapy or radiation. People heal themselves of cancer.

How do they do it? It's with their thought. If you put that light, that divine light on it and start thinking these good feeling thoughts instead of disease that then creates the cancer, it will disappear. What I do is I start creating ease with good feeling thoughts. Disease will become "ease" and that's what will happen for you. You will have ease and relaxation and tranquility and be feeling relaxed and joyful, feeling more freedom.

You don't need to read a diet book. You don't need to go on a diet, you don't need to pay attention. All you need is to pay attention to your feelings because your feelings are your guidance system, and it will guide you to the perfect food. As an example, every morning I have delicious and healthy food. Society doesn't put "delicious" and "healthy" together. The mass consciousness makes it sound like healthy food is awful tasting and delicious food is bad for you. I call forth that I can have delicious and healthy food. I can have them both. I can have it the way I want it and then eat it and have it be good for me.

Step Two: Breathe deeply

Whenever you can, breathe in about five seconds and then breathe out about five seconds. When you're driving along, sitting in front of your computer, walking down the stairs, going to your car, as often as you can breathe deeply.

Why? The fastest and easiest way to connect with your Source is through your breath. As you breathe deeply you will find a silence within you that is the core of your divinity. This divine silence is calling you to align to the vibration of your Source. As you breathe deeply and easily you fall into the lap of God as you are quiet, soft, and gentle, so this is the path, the lighted path to your oneness with God, and then to go out as you allow that in and you allow to be aligned with your Source.

As you go out into the world, everything becomes perfect like you. The perfect food shows up. The perfect people show up. The perfect opportunity shows up. Perfect manifestation shows up.

This is a perfect world we live in, but we have been taught the beliefs that make it imperfect. Thinking in silence, perfect. It's beautiful and you can feel it right now.

In the Bible, the word spirit actually means breath. Being conscious about our breath will keep us connected. Often what happens when we think something goes wrong, is we say, "Oh, no," and we stop breathing. Not breathing actually starts even more momentum towards something we don't want. There really isn't any good or bad, this is about wanted and unwanted. When I rub up against not wanted feelings, I point to them and say, "I don't want you." And, what does this birth? It takes me to the wanted feelings. Good feelings and breathing in deeply takes you right to your Source. Stop listening to this outside world that says, "You've got to be doing a lot." Going out there and doing a lot of stuff and getting it done and lots of action and all the struggles that go along with it–that's all upstream; that's all the world.

If you want to live in the world with this perfection, you must go in first and align yourself with whatever vibration (that beautiful love and compassion, soft, kind and quiet vibration) that is your Source within you. From there you will be guided out into the world to see the perfection of you and the world.

Step Three: Drink lots of water

Water allows the flow, the physical flow, between you and God. You're allowing that flow and that's one of the reasons there is no such thing as urinating too much. You're flowing, baby. It's great.

Stay on Your Lighted Path

In my book, *Good Feeling Thoughts,* there are seven good-feeling thoughts for each day of the year. We are trained for bad news. Turn on the TV if you don't believe me. Start watching the news. They search the world to find something bad that happened. My *Good Feeling Thoughts* book is helpful to train your mind to look for good! Using it offers an easy way to start attracting good things into your life.

You want to take control of what comes your way. You want to think about these good feeling thoughts, your good health, and your youthfulness. Think to yourself, "I'm getting younger every day." If you tell others about it, they'll try to pull you off your lighted path. They will try to take you from your train and put you on a mass consciousness train which is going uphill, not getting far and which isn't much fun.

Stay on your lighted path, it's a fun trip and you're going downhill. You are going to enjoy the train ride.

Epilogue

When I was growing up, my mother was afraid of my powerful, overwhelming, demanding, and commanding father. When he wasn't around, she actually did many things. For instance, she introduced me to yoga and breathing. We understand that in the Bible spirit means breath. By breathing deeply, we can connect quickly to our Source. She also was influenced by transcendental meditation.

Transcendental meditation taught me a little about meditation. At that time, I was a teenager. I was out having fun doing all the other things that I've described, the simple iconic 60s teen.

When I was in my early 20s, my mother became a practitioner for *Science of Mind*. She would send me tapes from a minister of *Science of Mind*. He mainly talked from his heart and about what he was channeling. It was interesting information that I hadn't been exposed to before.

Then the question came up, "Are you getting your information from mass consciousness or Source?" The answer was (and for all of us in varying degrees) we're getting information from our experience. That's from the world, and it can be mass consciousness.

Typically, mass consciousness is not engaged in the nonphysical. Instead mass consciousness is engaged with a physical reality; the "It's a tough world out there, and it's a struggle," kind of reality.

There are a few people not influenced by mass consciousness, but who instead are influenced by Source. My mother was influenced by different things coming from Source; Science of Mind, transcendental meditation, yoga, and breathing.

It's actually quite an influence as I reflect back on it. I was in Virginia for missile training, right out of basic training for the Army. I was on this guard stand; it was in the middle of nowhere. There was a large forest I was guarding. I was out in nature, above all the trees (almost like a bird) and I started to give a sermon. It was an amazing, amazing sermon, and I didn't know where the words were coming from.

That was the first time that I recognized and understood. I didn't have the word "channeling," but I understood that I was actually receiving information from Source. An energy form was turning into thoughts and coming out of my mouth as words.

It was an amazing awakening to realize that we can get our thoughts from different places. Whether it's from people who are connected with Source or mass consciousness that is out there. We can observe the things that are happening and tell that story, or we can channel and get our thoughts from this energy, from Source, that turns into thoughts that we then can turn into words.

About three years ago, I was introduced to Abraham, another influencer in my life. Abraham is part of creative intelligence that is channeled through Ester Hicks who is sharing this truth. Those influencers have been amazing. We can open these channels to receive and have the truth given to us.

I channel before a talk, I ask that Source have John F. Kennedy with me and other people who have walked before me who are engaged and have the experience. Since they are now pure Source and energy, they can give me their experience and flow through me.

I gave my first talk on turning challenges into opportunities. I called in for help. Thoughts and words came to me and out of me that I have never had before. The words flowed right from me, out to my audience. They were the perfect words for the people. In fact, I have the perfect emotions and thoughts. I have the perfect sensations, body language, the perfect tone of voice and the perfect words. It's because I asked for that, and I was given it.

Some of the things that we ask for can manifest immediately because we have little resistance. Some of them will take a while. For example, I am focused on really living the life of my soul, the life of my Source and to understand the true intent of why I'm here.

Overall, my true intent is for more joy, more happiness, and more freedom. Automatically, I'm going to get more growth.

The other thing is when I tune-in to what is happening. I tune-in to my soul, and I start living the life of my soul. There is nothing finer than the happiness that comes from the alignment with one's soul and it comes simply by asking for it.

Some things will come instantly to you, and some things suggest you be patient and know that the Universe is contriving to bring it to you; there are thousands of fingers right now weaving everything in the non-physical to bring you that experience that you're asking for.

By believing and being intentional, the thing I desire is to live the life of my soul. By doing that, my soul life creates all the happiness. I am no longer concerned with what my physical experience has done and what my thoughts have gotten from mass consciousness. Instead I believe and understand that I can get from creative intelligence from my soul, from my Source, everything that I want, whether it's a thought, feelings, circumstances, or situation into my life.

About the Author

Dr. Hank is a passionate man who helps others using a time proven success formula that taps into their unlimited potential, while guaranteeing specific and measurable business improvements.

He was a General Manager with Procter & Gamble (P&G) for 15 years, managing a billion-dollar business in the Southeast United States.

He developed a Success Formula for business success and used this process first with P&G and sales grew by 21%, and costs dropped by 34% in less than a year, while helping his people personally tap into their brilliance.

He left P&G and began his own consulting practice in 1995, with his first client being P&G. Since then he has served as an advisor to the Board of John Deere and helped Coca-Cola, IBM, Chase Bank, and hundreds of other large and small companies and entrepreneurs. All have achieved measurable business results and at least a 300% ROI.

Dr. Hank has a passion to help businesses grow and people to attain their greatest potential. He has helped hundreds of companies and thousands of people tap into their magnificence and achieve greater professional and personal achievement, along with using his productivity and hiring analytical system that increases productivity on average by 30% and retention by 50%. He has a degree in Business from the University of Wisconsin-Madison, and is a Behavioral and Talent Certified Analyst, with his PhD in Mental Science.

He is certified to administer the world's most statistically accurate and valid diagnostic tools that provide precision accuracy of people's behaviors, motivations, business acumen and talents. He is the creator of *"Top Performers"*, a time proven process that guarantees to increase your business or your investment is returned in full!

Sixteen years ago Dr. Hank broke his neck in a car accident and was in a coma where he was asked if he wanted to "stay or go" and he chose to stay. He opted not to have surgery to put a rod in his neck and instead put his faith in a great power. He was told he would have chronic pain for the rest of his life and once again he called upon his higher power and is now pain free and enjoying good health. From this he learned how all of us can overcome any obstacle in our lives and achieve all of our dreams by thinking good feeling thoughts and by only focusing on what we want and what we dream of being, doing and having.

Dr. Hank owns his consulting and coaching firm "Guaranteed Measurable Results", is a Partner in Ultima Real Estate with 380 agents in Texas, and has a factoring company that provides cash for companies that are in business, doing business. He has been called "The Spiritual Teacher" and likened to Santa Claus, carrying priceless gifts for others to enjoy as he helps people make their dreams come true!

Connect with Dr. Hank

Website: www.DrHank.biz
LinkedIn: http://www.linkedin.com/in/DrHankSeitz
Facebook: http://www.facebook.com/DrHankSeitz
Twitter: @DrHankSeitz
Instagram: @drhankseitz
Email: DrHank@DrHank.biz

www.ingramcontent.com/pod-product-compliance
Lightning Source LLC
Chambersburg PA
CBHW060047230426
43661CB00004B/691